Revolutionizing Education In America

The TOTIL Method

DORIS LECLERC BALL, Ph.D.

iUniverse, Inc.
Bloomington

Revolutionizing Education in America
The TOTIL Method

iUniverse books may be ordered through booksellers or by contacting:

iUniverse
1663 Liberty Drive
Bloomington, IN 47403
www.iuniverse.com
1-800-Authors (1-800-288-4677)

Because of the dynamic nature of the Internet, any web addresses or links contained in this book may have changed since publication and may no longer be valid. The views expressed in this work are solely those of the author and do not necessarily reflect the views of the publisher, and the publisher hereby disclaims any responsibility for them.

Any people depicted in stock imagery provided by Thinkstock are models, and such images are being used for illustrative purposes only.

Certain stock imagery © Thinkstock.

ISBN: 978-1-4620-3224-2 (sc)
ISBN: 978-1-4620-3225-9 (e)
ISBN: 978-1-4620-3226-6 (dj)

Printed in the United States of America

iUniverse rev. date: 8/4/2011

To the men in my life:

my husband, George

and

my sons, Timothy and Eric

who have supported me in all my endeavors

Table of Contents

Acknowledgments

First, I would like to thank Spencer Axline Ball, my grandson. Spencer was my inspiration and my research subject. He taught me more than I taught him—that the Independent Learning (IL) method is possible with very young children. Spencer's cooperative attitude and enthusiasm made him an ideal student and research subject.

The contribution of the late Jacob Kounin, Ph.D. was also important to this work. Dr. Kounin helped me to realize the enormous difference between Time on Task and time spent "schooling" (my term, not his), time spent in school, studying or pretending to study.

Thanks are also owed for editorial work to George Ball, Timothy Sams, Ph.D. and Eric Ball, Ph.D., who reviewed the manuscript and offered numerous, helpful suggestions.

Introduction

Americans have known for decades that their educational system is in serious trouble. Their students do not compare favorably with students from many other countries, especially in basic subjects such as math and science. I believe that my particular combination of teaching experience, academic experience and research in education and psychology gives me a unique background to offer a solution to this problem. The most essential of these qualifications is my extensive teaching experience. Even more important than helping me to understand what a teacher can accomplish, this experience taught me what a teacher cannot accomplish. This knowledge encouraged me to look beyond accepted solutions and to promote a total revamping of our educational system through a change in educational methodology from the teacher-centered method to the learner-centered method.

Shortly after I received my B.A. in foreign languages and social studies from Wayne State University in Detroit, Michigan and a permanent teaching certificate for the public schools of Michigan, I began teaching in the public schools of Detroit at all levels—elementary school, middle school and high school. Within two years, I accepted a position in a public high school in an affluent suburb of Detroit.

After many years of teaching, I realized that no matter how enthusiastically I taught or how I varied or improved my teaching techniques, my students did not learn nearly as much as they should have been learning in my classes. Even worse, their preparation for the demands of my classes deteriorated steadily over the years and I was eventually compelled to "dumb down" my exams. Most of my colleagues were complaining about these same issues and attributed these problems to a lack of discipline and industry on the part of students.

Eventually, I concluded that, if I were a principal, I would have the authority to make disciplinary, curricular and methodological changes that could lead to a better education for students. Consequently, I attended the University of Michigan to acquire an M.A. in educational administration. However, shortly after I acquired my administrative degree, I realized that principals have no real authority in such areas. Superintendents and members of the board of education do not have a great deal of authority either. Ultimately, most decision-making authority over school districts resides with judges and other government officials.

Finally, after more than twenty years of teaching, I admitted to myself that my efforts would probably never make a significant difference in student performance and that I was no longer receiving the satisfaction I needed to continue. Therefore, although I had a good relationship with my students and was not eager to leave them, I decided to become a clinical psychologist. As a result, I returned to graduate school and acquired an M.A. in psychology from Oakland University in Oakland, Michigan and a Ph.D. in clinical and educational psychology from Wayne State University in Detroit, Michigan. However, I did not stop teaching.

For approximately 20 years, as a cognitive-behavioral clinical psychologist, I taught clients to change their behavior, and, to a lesser extent, alter their thinking, to overcome significant problems that were negatively impacting their lives. My last position before I retired was teaching psychology to physician residents. I was a member of the faculty and Director of Psychology at Beaumont Hospital in Troy, Michigan. I assumed this would be a more successful teaching experience than my high school teaching experience because the physician residents were more mature and more motivated to learn. It was not. Apparently, learning requires more than maturation and motivation. For example, it also requires solitude, more visual presentation, especially the printed word, and time for the brain to absorb and process the information being presented.

The primary target audience for *Revolutionizing Education in America: The TOTIL Method* is parents of children who are presently attending school or intending to do so, whether it is public school or private school, including parochial school. A secondary target audience is parents of homeschooled children. The latter will have less difficulty accepting the TOTIL method because they have already begun to make the most important adjustment necessary to implement this method. They have greatly reduced their dependence on teachers. However, they need to understand how TOTIL is different from homeschooling and how they and their children can profit significantly from this difference. A tertiary target audience is people who are paying for the education of children, whether they are taxpayers, parents of children attending private schools, or both.

My decision to become a teacher was based on my belief that very few pursuits are more important than education, whether it is gained through books or experience. Education is the road to understanding the world around us, an improved quality of life and financial success. Helping others to learn was, in my opinion, an extremely important and satisfying goal. Unfortunately, I did not realize that there is a significant difference between helping others to learn and teaching others. The former is extremely productive and constructive, while the latter, especially in an academic context, is usually destructive, academically and psychologically. We cannot significantly improve the quality of education until we change from the teacher-centered method to the learner-centered method.

Revolutionizing Education in America: The TOTIL Method describes my journey to discover the most effective and efficient method of education possible. I believe I have accomplished this goal. Try the TOTIL method and judge for yourself.

Chapter 1
Time on Task

E ducation in America is in crisis. Now. We must act. Now. No more procrastination. No more first aid. We cannot continue to put band-aids on a seriously infected, deep wound. The patient will soon die. In many cases, he or she already has. We cannot improve our children's education until we change our entire philosophy of education, including our basic assumptions about educational objectives and educational methodology. We must begin by rejecting the myths that are being perpetuated about effective teaching and learning. To start, we must discover the most important variables for a superior education. This knowledge will provide the solution to the problem.

Many research studies have been conducted to discover which variables are most important and to what degree. The most common variables thought to correlate with student performance include: expenditure per student, teacher education, classroom discipline, teacher enthusiasm, parental involvement, number of students per class, socio-economic class of the students, IQ of students, type and/or quality of the school, public, private, parochial, etc.

Most educational researchers, parents and government officials have believed for many years that the most important variable in educational success is the amount of expenditure per child. This assumption has been discredited. Quality of education in the United States is at an all-time low compared to numerous other countries even though expenditures for education by the United States are at an all-time high compared to other countries. According to the *Programme for International Student Assessment* (PISA) tests for 2009, the United States ranked thirtieth in math, twenty-fourth in sciences and seventeenth in reading out of sixty-five countries tested.[1] However, the United States ranked second highest in the amount of expenditure per child out of twenty-eight OECD (Organization for Economic Co-operation and Development) countries.[2] Apparently, expenditure per child is not the most important variable for a superior education as has usually been assumed. Then what is?

In the 1970's, Jacob Kounin, Ph.D., an educational researcher and professor at Wayne State University in Detroit, Michigan, decided to conduct a research study to discover the most important variables for effective classroom learning. To accomplish this, he sent graduate students with television cameras into numerous classrooms. These graduate students had been carefully trained in Dr. Kounin's method to ensure consistency in data collection. They spent over one thousand hours televising students and teachers. Since the study was conducted in the Detroit area, it was quite easy to control for socio-economic factors because the researchers could easily get to either the inner-city schools or the more affluent northern suburbs.

From his research, Dr. Kounin concluded that, while many of the variables mentioned in previous educational studies contributed to improved learning, classroom discipline by the teacher was, by far, the single most important variable of all. Dr. Kounin wrote a book entitled *Discipline and Group Management in Classrooms* in which he discussed his research study and his conclusions.

During my graduate studies, I attended a class in educational psychology at Wayne State University. Dr. Kounin was the professor for this class. On the last day of the course, Dr. Kounin discussed his well-known research study and stated that he still believed that classroom discipline was essential for superior learning. However, he now realized that this was because classroom discipline, and all other variables that had been found by other researchers to be important, had one element in common: increased Time on Task (TOT). I have observed, tested and confirmed the primacy of Time on Task for mastery of new information many times. Dr. Kounin had, indeed, found *the* essential variable for a superior education. I am indebted to Dr. Kounin for coalescing my thinking on this critical issue.

How does classroom discipline relate to Time on Task? Whenever a student is disruptive, it distracts other students and the teacher for some period of time and decreases Time on Task. My husband's grandfather, George, was a farmer who hired young teenage boys to work for him. He used to say, "If you have one boy, you have a boy. If you have two boys, you have half a boy. If you have three boys, you have no boy at all." Therefore, Grandpa George gave all his hired help chores on different parts of the farm so that they would not interact and be distracted from their chores. This indicates that, in a classroom setting, for the best performance, the teacher must keep all student interaction to an absolute minimum. However, minimizing student interaction is extremely difficult, and as I will discuss later, totally contrary to the present progressive/social philosophy of education.

Teachers with good classroom discipline can often predict which stimuli are likely to elicit disruptive behavior and avoid them, or, once such behavior begins, can stop it quickly. Preventing disruption in the classroom means that teachers have to be totally involved, energetic and vigilant every minute. After a few hours, they are usually quite exhausted and the later classes do not get the same quality of teaching as do the earlier classes. How soon teachers become exhausted, mentally and physically, depends to a large extent, not only on how energetic they are, but also on how many disruptive students they have in each class. It only takes one or two disrupters in each class to produce teacher burnout very quickly.

The main reason it is so difficult for a teacher to keep all students involved in the learning process is because learning in this manner, that is, the teacher-centered method, is, by definition, a passive enterprise for students, not an active one, and when students are bored, they become distracted, and then, either disruptive or withdrawn. However, trying to counteract student boredom by having students and teachers interact, leads to even more distraction and less Time on Task.

After many years of teaching and just as many in research on education, I have concluded that there is one variable that leads to the most Time on Task possible—even more important than classroom management—learner-centered education, that is Independent Learning

(IL). With this method there are no teachers, no other students, no distractions and much, much more Time on Task. A synonym for these two terms is "studying." More on this in Chapter 6.

Considering that Time on Task is the most important single variable for achieving a superior education, a closer examination of this variable is warranted. Fortunately, the importance of Time on Task has been well documented by Malcolm Gladwell in his book, *Outliers: the Story of Success,* one of the most interesting and insightful books I have read for some time. The main theme of Gladwell's book is that success can be explained better in terms of generation, family, culture, and economic class, that is, luck, than by intelligence and ambition. However, Gladwell also believes strongly that Time on Task is necessary to take advantage of this luck when it appears. In other words, "the harder one works, the luckier one gets," or, the more prepared one is, the more likely s/he will be able to catch the brass ring when it appears.

Gladwell states that there is a consensus among researchers that approximately ten thousand hours is the optimal number of hours of focused attention and/or performance needed to achieve mastery or expertise in almost anything. Without such Time on Task, other important variables such as ambition, energy, ability, intelligence, luck, etc., are not likely to lead to optimal success. Gladwell gives several very interesting examples to prove his point. I will mention just three: Bill Gates, The Beatles, and Chinese wet-rice farmers.

My assumption, and perhaps that of others, was that Bill Gates was a very intelligent young man from a reasonably wealthy family who went to Harvard; became interested in computers; stumbled into a new idea involving computers; and with a little ambition, family support and entrepreneurial skill parlayed this idea into a multi-billion dollar corporation. While this scenario is partially true, a very important factor has been ignored: Time on Task.

A brief look at Gates' background, taken from Gladwell's book, is in order. When Gates was in the eighth grade, he and a group of friends started a computer club and convinced some of the parents to acquire a computer that was a time-sharing terminal with a direct link to a mainframe computer in downtown Seattle. This was in 1968 when almost all other computers operated with a very slow computer-card system. Gates and several friends spent every hour possible in the computer room programming and teaching themselves to use this intriguing new invention.

Some time later, Gates and his friends began spending time at the University of Washington and, in exchange for computer work, earned free computer time. After this job ended, Gates and his friend, Paul, found a computer at the Medical Center and Physics Department of the University of Washington that was not being used between three and six in the morning. Gates and Paul would sneak out of bed after their parents were asleep and go to the university to steal time on their computer. Later, when Gates was in his senior year in high school, he was hired by a technology company called TRW that was setting up a computer system at the Bonneville Power Station in Washington State.

Gladwell states that, "In one seven-month period in 1971, Gates and his cohorts ran up 1,575 hours of computer time on the ISI (Information Sciences, Inc.) mainframe. This averages out to eight hours a day, seven days a week." From the eighth grade through his senior year in high school, Gates amassed thousands of hours in learning to program computers before he went to Harvard. Time on Task.

Another Gladwell example of Time on Task that lead to enormous success is from the experience of the musical group, The Beatles. In 1960, The Beatles, a not-especially-talented high school band from Liverpool, England, accepted a job from Bruno, the owner of a nightclub in Hamburg, Germany. Bruno's club offered a huge nonstop show with bands that would play constantly to catch the in-and-out traffic.

At Bruno's club and others in Hamburg, The Beatles, who were used to playing only their best songs over and over again in one-hour sessions were required to play eight hours a night, seven nights a week. According to Gladwell, by the time The Beatles appeared in New York in February of 1965, they had performed twelve hundred times, which is more than most bands play in their entire careers. According to Philip Norman, who wrote The Beatles' biography, *Shout*, "They were no good onstage when they went there [Hamburg] and they were very good when they came back." Time on Task.

Just one more example of the results of Time on Task from *Outliers*, and perhaps the most important one for purposes of this book, will help to explain the success of an entire ethnic group—the Chinese.

In *Outliers,* Gladwell attributes the legendary work ethic of ethnic Chinese to their cultural legacy of extremely hard work in the unusually labor-intensive task of wet-rice farming. According to Gladwell, "Some estimates put the annual workload of a wet-rice farmer in China at *three thousand* hours a year." This cultural legacy of hard work by the farmers in China spread to other countries of East Asia: Korea, Singapore, Taiwan and Japan, and may help to explain the present academic success of students from most of the major Asian nations.[3] Most continue to act as their ancestors did. They have maintained the ethic of hard work and long hours, which is their cultural heritage.

Several years ago, when my granddaughter was attending middle school in Irvine, California, I told my daughter-in-law about my theory of Time on Task. Months later Lari came to me and said that she agreed with me about Time on Task. When I asked why, she explained that a large percentage of the students in my granddaughter's middle school were ethnic Chinese and that almost all appeared to be very high achievers. One day Lari spoke to a Chinese parent at a social gathering and asked her why she thought Chinese students seemed to do so much better than non-Chinese students in academic settings. The parent said, "extra work." Then she explained that most Chinese parents insist that their children spend extra time outside of school on their academic or skill subjects, such as math or piano. She commented that one half-hour more per day amounts to over 100 extra hours per year. Time on Task.

To further demonstrate the importance of Time on Task, I will examine the success of a recognized, academically-superior charter school in the United States highlighted in the movie *Waiting for Superman.* The main theme of this movie is that public school teachers and teacher unions are to blame for the present poor condition of public education. Another theme is that, while regular public schools are bad, charter schools are good, even though the movie pointed out that fewer than one in five charter schools are performing better than regular public schools. This movie shows the angst of parents who must win a lottery for admission of their children to charter schools because they are overcrowded.

Much has been written about this academically exceptional college preparatory public charter school in the South Bronx in New York

City called KIPP (Knowledge Is Power Program) Academy Middle School. This school was begun in 1994 in a fifth grade class in inner-city Houston, Texas, by two teachers, Mike Feinberg and Dave Levin. Levin left Houston in 1995 to establish another branch of the school in the Bronx. Currently there are approximately one hundred KIPP schools throughout the country. An examination of the special characteristics of these schools is warranted to help determine what factors might explain their phenomenal success.[4] KIPP students made dramatic gains on the 2009 California API standardized tests and KIPP schools were the recipient of the National Excellence in Urban Education Award.[5]

The primary objective of KIPP is "to ensure that our students develop the academic skills, intellectual habits, and character traits needed to succeed in top-quality high schools, colleges, and the competitive world beyond."[6] Feinberg and Levin attribute much of the success of KIPP to its outstanding teachers who receive regular training and professional development throughout the school year through the KIPP Foundation. Teachers exchange lesson plans and gain new skills to improve their classroom practice. Feinberg and Levin also stress the importance of strict discipline and extra Time on Task.[7]

Students at KIPP attend school from 7:30 a.m. to 5:00 p.m. each week day, half a day on selected Saturdays, and an extra month in the summer. They are also expected to do two to three hours of homework each evening. According to KIPP research, this amounts to sixty percent more Time on Task than students are required to do in other public or private schools.[8]

As stated above, in KIPP schools a great deal of emphasis is placed on discipline. Both rewards and punishments are used. One form of discipline is called "benching." In benching, students are isolated for a day. As a result, they are not even allowed to eat with other students. As a reward for good behavior or academic achievement students receive a paycheck at the end of the week in KIPP dollars. With these dollars they can buy end-of-the-year trips, including trips to Washington, D.C., Utah, the East coast or the West Coast. KIPP administrators believe that this concept will generalize outside the classroom. Children will learn that they are not entitled to anything. They get things because they earn them.[9]

KIPP schools, like other charter schools, receive much less funding from the districts than do regular public schools, and they usually spend less per student than do larger school districts, even though teachers receive larger salaries. The reason for the larger salaries of KIPP teachers is that they work many more hours per year than do other public school or private school teachers.[10]

Can the above description of KIPP schools help us to determine which characteristic(s) of KIPP schools might account for their extraordinary success? It is obviously not due to superior I.Q. because the students are not screened. It is not due to the advantages of economic class because over eighty percent of the students are from low-income families. It is not due to past achievement because entering students are usually one to two grades below grade level. It is not due to more money from the government because they get less.[11] Given my own experience, I am not inclined to give much credit to the ongoing training and development of KIPP teachers or any other teachers. I have found "teacher days" to be mostly a waste of time, a day off. While it is possible that some teachers may get some minor benefit from hints from other teachers about particular techniques on how to teach a particular concept or how to improve discipline, I do not believe that it is really possible to teach someone else to be a better teacher. More importantly, while further teacher education may make teachers more educated, academically and/or pedagogically, this is not the preferred goal. The preferred goal is to educate students, not teachers, that is, to use a learner-centered approach, not a teacher-centered approach.

Regarding the difficulty of teaching someone to be a good teacher, my own experience is a good example. When I was a college student I was looking forward to the few education classes I would take to become a credentialed teacher so that someone would teach me how to teach. This did not happen. In education classes, we talked about child psychology, educational psychology, the management of the school, etc., but nothing about how to teach the subject or how or when to discipline students.

Once I realized that I was not going to get any help in teacher education classes, I assumed I would get it during my student teaching internship from the acknowledged superior teacher to whom I was assigned. Ms. Howard allowed me to watch her teach a class for two days.

Then on the third day she said to me, "O.K., do it."

"Do what"? I asked, perplexed.

"Teach the class," she replied.

Now, imagine yourself in exactly the same predicament. What would you do? How would you start? I'm sure you know from personal experience that it is very difficult to control just three or four children who are together. Now, imagine that you not only have to control thirty boisterous students sitting closely together, you also have to teach them. Exactly how would you proceed? If you don't think you could do it, what makes you think teachers can do a good job of it?

Ms. Howard watched as I taught.

Afterwards, I asked, "How did I do?"

"Fantastic," she replied. "It would have taken me a week to cover that much material."

I was flattered for about three seconds until I realized that she was telling me that I had gone much too fast. That was the last comment or criticism she ever made relative to my teaching style or methods. The point is, I had to learn for myself—or not. Teaching is not a skill that can be taught.

"Teacher days" are comparable to required education classes for continued credentialing for other professionals, such as psychologists or medical doctors. These professionals usually select a course in a pleasant, vacation-oriented locale, spend a few hours in class, and then hit the slopes in a nice ski resort or escape to a golf course. Professionals who want to update or improve their skills or knowledge do it on their own.

If I do not give much credit for the superior success of KIPP schools to the ongoing training and development of their teachers, then to what do I attribute the dramatic success of KIPP schools? Time on Task. Consider that, as has been stated above, students have a twelve-hour day. All in all, they spend sixty percent more Time on Task than in a regular public or private school. In addition, due to the better behavior of fellow students because of their strict discipline, they are less distracted which leads to even more Time on Task.

Of course, the motivation of teachers and students, which leads to their willingness to spend nine to twelve hours a day involved in teaching and learning, is very important to the success of KIPP and other such schools. Part of this motivation may be due to the "Hawthorne Effect" whereby improvement occurs because the people involved know they are part of an experiment and they feel special, so they work harder. A larger part of the motivation is probably due to the fact that both the parents and the children recognize that the extra time and effort in KIPP may be the only way for them to break free of their present grim situation and build a much more successful life than their parents had or than they could reach without such effort. It is likely that this would not work as well in less disadvantaged areas where children have more opportunities.

The improved behavior of the students at KIPP and their willingness to work much harder may be due, in part, to the fact that they are self selected (or parent selected). Attrition in KIPP schools is higher than average in the first few years that a KIPP school is open. After that it declines and is much lower than for surrounding district schools.[12] I believe this is because some students have opted out and others do not opt in because they know what is expected and are not willing or able to devote that much time and/or effort to school. Those who are there want to be there. They are highly motivated to perform, and almost as important, so are their parents. It is important to recognize that little can be accomplished without significant support from parents.

At this point, I need to differentiate between Time on Task and "schooling." Time on Task refers to the amount of time actually spent on studying, that is, on mentally attending only to the lesson, which means time spent on processing information. Schooling refers to time spent on school related activities, including: time spent in school interacting with others, daydreaming, lunch, recess, seeing the counselor, or attending sports rallies; or at home or school pretending to study or actually studying.

I assume that the twelve hours a day spent in schooling in a KIPP school or the twelve-fifteen hours a day schooling spent in most Asian schools would lead to more Time on Task than a regular six hour American school if all other factors are equal, especially the use of the teacher-centered group method.

The reward for spending sixty-seventy percent more time in schooling in a KIPP school or Asian school is better mastery of academic and performance subjects. But, is it worth it? And, are these our only choices? Or, is there a better alternative? Yes, there is a better alternative: spending the same amount of time as is spent in schooling in a regular public or private American school (six hours per day) but getting results similar to a KIPP or Asian school, which devotes twelve-fifteen hours per day to schooling. This is the TOTIL method. More on this later.

Chapter 2
Factors That Contribute
to Time on Task

I t is important to examine the variables that are generally considered to be important for a superior education. It will become clear that these variables are important only to the extent that they add to Time on Task and that Time on Task is the overriding determinant of a superior education.

Since most people, especially those in government education agencies, promote the idea that money is the essential ingredient for a superior education, we will examine this premise first, in more detail than previously mentioned. *Program for International Student Assessment* (PISA) scores on the 2003 tests for twenty-nine countries were compared to determine if countries that spent more on education did better on the tests. They did not. For example, the United States scored poorly, twenty-fourth out of twenty-nine countries in math on the 2003 tests, although it spent much more than most of the other countries.[13] In addition, according to data from the Organization for Economic Co-operation and Development (OECD) from the 2009 PISA tests, the United States ranked thirtieth in math, twenty-third in science and seventeenth in reading out of sixty-five countries, but was second out of twenty-eight OECD countries in expenditure per child. These data are presented in Table 1.

Table 1: K-12 Spending Per Student in the OECD Countries in 2009* (average per year over nine years)	
1. Switzerland	$10,367
2. United States	$10,189
3. Norway	$ 9,700
4. Austria	$ 9,589
5. Iceland	$ 9,300
6. Denmark	$ 8,667
7. Italy	$ 8,333
8. Sweden	$ 8,033
9. Belgium	$ 7,811
10. Japan	$ 7,667
11. Netherlands	$ 7,411
12. France	$ 7,333
13. Finland	$ 7,111
14. United Kingdom	$ 7,056
15.Australia	$ 7,033
16. Ireland	$ 6,344
17. Spain	$ 6,256
18. Germany	$ 6,244
19. Portugal	$ 5,889
20. Korea	$ 5,878
21. New Zealand	$ 5,811
22. Greece	$ 5,333
23. Czech Republic	$ 4,189
24. Hungary	$ 4,078
25. Poland	$ 3,411
26. Slovak Republic	$ 2,589
27. Mexico	$ 1,856
28.Turkey	$ 1,367[14]

Another 2009 research study by the Heritage Foundation also indicates that amount of money spent per child has been found to have very little, if any, correlation to children's school performance. The authors noted that "Continuous spending increases have not corresponded with equal improvement in American educational performance. Increasing federal funding on education has not been followed by similar gains in student achievement."[15] We must realize that money spent per child is primarily money spent on salaries for teachers, administrators and support staff, as well as on buildings, swimming pools, auditoriums, gymnasiums and football fields.

Many researchers have suggested that parental interest and/or input is an important variable for a superior education. This is a reasonable assumption. A more interested, involved parent will usually supervise, or at least check, that their child has completed school assignments; see that the child is not absent from school unnecessarily; and/or offer enrichment opportunities, such as providing books or other educational resources for use in the home. Time on Task.

Socio-economic class (SES) has also been found to be an important variable in effective learning, but only as it relates to Time on Task. If children do not have to work to earn money, they have more time and energy for study. Also, during summer vacations and other vacations, children from upper socioeconomic classes are exposed to numerous advantages, especially books, but also travel, which is very educational, and various academic and non-academic "camps" that offer numerous educational opportunities. This premise is affirmed by Gladwell. In *Outliers*, he suggests that children from the upper socioeconomic class do better because of how they spend their time outside of school.

Several important research studies have shown that, while children of equivalent IQ's may begin Kindergarten or first grade with relatively similar levels of advancement in math and reading, within a few years, there is usually a vast difference of several grade levels in their performance. This is because they lose ground over the summer because they are not exposed to books and other educational advantages mentioned above. This indicates that programs such as pre-Kindergarten and Head Start will not have a lasting advantage.[16]

In the 2009 PISA tests, in all countries, students scored better if their parents were higher earners.[17] This was a separate finding from the socio-economic finding but is probably related.

Some researchers have suggested that the poor performance in PISA tests by the United States may be a result of its heterogeneous population. An analysis of the 2006 PISA data suggests that the poor ranking of students from the United States is not a result of the inclusion of scores from immigrant or disadvantaged or minority students. A comparatively small percentage of white students were high achievers in these tests.[18]

Analysis of the data from the 2006 PISA tests also indicates that even the children of college educated parents in the United States do not perform well on these tests compared with students in a majority of OECD countries.[19]

PISA tests for 2009 did not include homeschooled students, only students attending school.[20] It would be very interesting to compare PISA test results of homeschooled students with students who attend school to ascertain if homeschoolers are better educated as many have claimed.

A variable that is rarely mentioned, but quite important for educational success, is peer pressure or family expectations. Children whose family or friends expect them to go to college are more likely to do so, especially if the example is set. In some families or schools, for example, one student will often ask another, "What college are you going to go to?" or "What college did you apply to?" instead of, "Are you going to college?" or "What are you going to do after you graduate from high school?" People, especially young people, are usually easily influenced, especially if "everybody" is doing it.

Smaller class size does not appear to affect student performance significantly. If we assume that Time on Task is the single, most important variable in effective learning (which, of course, I do), then the next question should be: What is the optimal number of students that should be in a class? Reverting to the advice of Grandpa George: "One boy is a boy, two boys are half a boy, and three boys are no boy at all," the obvious answer would appear to be one student per class. That sounds suspiciously like homeschooling or some reasonable equivalent. Yes, but with some important twists. More on this later.

The most important variables, which are rarely mentioned, that lead to an individual's willingness to devote more Time on Task to education or other pursuits, are his or her over-all philosophy of life and character traits, or those of the culture from which he or she came. This includes a sense of personal responsibility, a willingness to work hard to attain goals and a personal philosophy regarding the goal of education or training. All this is dependent upon an individual's psychological orientation (internal or external). Internal orientation means that you believe that you are capable of doing what you need to do to survive and improve your life, and that you believe it is up to you as to whether or not you will succeed. External orientation means that you believe that you are not capable of doing what you need to do to survive, that is, that your survival is out of your control. Internal orientation enabled the Chinese in the rice paddies, the colonists on the American frontier and numerous other individuals to survive and prosper.

A good example of internal orientation can be found in a large research study I conducted that attempted to determine why one person would be successful at ceasing their dependence on a drug, such as nicotine, while another would not be successful. This was accomplished by dividing 364 smokers into three groups: those who had never smoked; those who had smoked for at least a year and had tried to quit smoking but were unsuccessful; and those who had smoked for at least a year and who had successfully quit, that is, had been free of nicotine for at least a year.

The aim of the research was to discover if there were habits or traits within the individuals that could be used to distinguish and predict which individuals were likely to be able to quit smoking from those who were not likely to be able to quit. The study was extremely successful. It predicted, with a ninety-five percent confidence level, which smokers would likely be able to quit smoking and which would not.

I discovered fifteen variables that could be used to make this determination. However, upon close examination, these variables were reduced to one primary variable: the degree of confidence the smoker had at the beginning of the attempt in his or her ability to be able to stop smoking, that is, whether or not the smoker was internally oriented or externally oriented. Or, as succinctly stated in a quote attributed to Henry Ford, "Whether you think you can, or whether you think you can't, you're right either way." This, of course, is similar in principle to the fact that most or all variables related to a superior academic education can be reduced to Time on Task.

Gladwell quotes some Chinese proverbs which indicate clearly that their personal philosophies and character traits of self-reliance, independence and internal orientation contribute greatly to their success.

"No food without blood and sweat."

"In winter, the lazy man freezes to death."

"Don't depend on heaven for food, but on your own two hands carrying the load."

"Useless to ask about the crops, it all depends on hard work and fertilizer."

"If a man works hard, the land will not be lazy."

"No one who can rise before dawn three hundred sixty days a year fails to make his family rich."

To reiterate the above: it is obvious that the most important factor necessary for an individual to be willing to expend considerable Time on Task is a personal philosophy that believes that you alone are responsible for your own success or failure. Then, you must have the confidence that you can do what it takes to succeed or, at least, the knowledge that you are willing to try. One last example of this is the story of a remarkable woman, Mrs. Georgina Leclerc.

Mrs. Leclerc was a French Canadian mother of eight children who, like many other Canadians in 1941, was extremely interested in immigrating to the United States with her children to obtain better work opportunities for them. Jobs were very difficult to get at that time in Ontario, and the best were given to English Canadians. However, immigration was almost impossible. Many of her relatives had been trying to accomplish this for years.

One day, Mrs. Leclerc's sister-in-law, Alice, asked Mrs. Leclerc if she would accompany her to the United States Immigration Office on the American side of the border with Michigan. Mrs. Leclerc agreed. After Alice had inquired about the possibility of immigrating with her family and had been told this was relatively impossible, Mrs. Leclerc casually asked if there was anything she could ever do to immigrate with her children.

"Where was your husband born?" asked the immigration officer.

"He was born in New York State and I was born in Michigan," she replied.

"Well then," the immigration officer replied, "your children are already citizens of the United States and can immigrate any time they want to by just crossing the border."

Shocked, Mrs. Leclerc replied, "No, you do not understand, the children were all born in Canada."

"Doesn't matter," he said, "If their father was born in America, they have been American citizens since the day they were born."

Still unable to believe her ears or the miracle that was occurring, Mrs. Leclerc tried again to get him to understand her situation. "But my husband and I have lived in Canada for over 30 years and the children have always lived there."

Probably somewhat irritated by this point, the officer tried again, "Lady, your children are all Americans, and so are you if you were born in Michigan, and you can all walk across the border anytime you want to and live here in the U.S."

Mrs. Leclerc walked home in the rain for almost two miles because she was crying too hard to take the streetcar. Six days later, she and her children, wearing several layers of clothing (because she was still sure she would be stopped by the immigration officers at the border), and clutching thirty-five dollars and no suitcases, they arrived in Detroit, Michigan, almost four hundred miles away.

A month later, after they had found a place to live, a social worker appeared at Mrs. Leclerc's door. The social worker said she had been told that Mrs. Leclerc had seven underage children and no husband or other means of support, and that the government was willing to give her a welfare check every month for more than one hundred dollars, which seemed like a fortune in 1941. Mrs. Leclerc was quite agitated.

"No," she said, "I will not let you ruin my children. If we take money from the government, they will take it away from us if any of my children work, so they will not work and we will soon become dependant and will never improve our situation."

"But madam," the social worker said, "without the checks, the children will starve."

"Then, they will starve," Mrs Leclerc replied, "or they will learn to work."

At that time, the oldest child in the family was an 18-year-old girl who had graduated as valedictorian from a five-year high school in Canada, which was equivalent to two years of college in the United States. The two oldest boys had attended technical school in Canada, but had not graduated. One was not old enough to have graduated yet and the other had entered the work force. The other five children were still in school, from first grade to eighth grade. Mrs. Leclerc's major focus was her children's education, although, or perhaps because, she had only attended school to the fourth grade.

All the children, except the four youngest, worked very hard at whatever jobs they could find and the family survived. Eventually, each of the members of the family became successful, hard-working adults who supported themselves and contributed more than they took from society. In my opinion, this would not have been the case if Mrs. Leclerc had accepted those welfare checks when they first arrived in the United States. But she believed in self-reliance and personal responsibility, as did the Chinese wet-rice farmers and the immigrants in colonial America. She was the wisest, most admirable person I have ever met. She was my mother.

I firmly believe that people who are given welfare and other "freebies" are being victimized. They are being infantilized and made dependent, usually for life. As a result, they do not believe that they alone are responsible for their lives, nor do they believe that they are capable of doing what is necessary to survive or improve their lives, as did Mrs. Leclerc and the Chinese wet-rice farmers. All the families who lived on the same street we did when my mother refused those welfare checks were still there twenty years later—accepting welfare checks.

It is very arrogant of the providers of welfare to assume that, without their magnanimous help, poor people would not be able to survive. I realize that much of the responsibility for the victimization belongs to the victims, themselves, and so, I am not solely blaming the givers.

Charity is another matter, of course. Both the giver and the taker understand that charity is temporary and voluntary and it does not create the same sense of entitlement that is so detrimental to everyone concerned. The road to Hell is paved with the givers' good intentions—if they are good intentions.

A corollary to Time on Task is time away from task. In other words, it is counterproductive to have much time spent away from the subject one is studying. Most learning is hierarchical and the flow is lost if the student stops for too long. Also, students forget previously learned concepts after a period of time and must relearn them. It is clear, therefore, that it would be best to have learning periods six days a week, instead of five, and not to have long vacations, especially two-month vacations in the summer. This also applies to any skill an individual is attempting to learn. If a individual wishes to learn to swim or to ski, for example, the closer together the lessons are taken or practice is done, the more quickly learning will take place and be retained.

In sum, most of the above variables are important to the quality of education only to the extent they contribute to Time on Task.

Chapter 3
Objectives of Education

What are the objectives of education in the United States? Unfortunately, the two fundamental objectives are mostly contradictory. From the early 20th century until the present, the primary objective for American public schools and most private schools has been to socialize the child – to prepare him/her to live in a democratic society according to the political beliefs of the leaders of the progressive movement in education. According to the expressed beliefs of the major proponents of this movement, such as Francis Parker, George Counts and John Dewey (the Father of Progressive Education), these aims can best be accomplished in a group setting with much student and teacher interaction. More on this later, including citations. This is the educational philosophy that was strongly emphasized and followed in all of the public school districts in which I taught for over twenty years, although it was rarely labeled as such. In many private, parochial or home schools, the primary objective is to educate the children in the social mores and religious beliefs of their parents.

The secondary objective of education in American public and most private schools is usually to prepare the child with the knowledge and ability necessary for financial success and self-fulfillment as an adult. However, as will be shown later, this requires study without the distraction of interacting with others and, therefore, is in conflict with the primary, social objective.

To acquire as much knowledge as possible for success and self-fulfillment students need to progress at their own pace according to their own ability. This is rarely accomplished. Many schools and teachers claim to have a program for gifted students so that the student can move at his/her own pace. This rarely involves moving a student up a grade level. It is feared that such a move would hurt the child socially more than it would help him or her academically and this may be true. The younger child might be picked on by the others for being a "nerd" and then made the butt of jokes and other bullying techniques, probably both psychological and physical. Many students deliberately underperform so that this does not happen to them.

Helping a student to move at his/her own pace usually involves some sort of enrichment program. This usually means the student will be given extra assignments, which very often are just busy work assignments with little academic value, for example, building a model of the Alamo in addition to merely studying about the Alamo. (This was an actual assignment for students in a middle school in Irvine, California). I have never yet seen an enrichment program that actually allowed students to move at their own pace. Do you really think a teacher has enough time and energy to handle a class of twenty-thirty students and give meaningful, individual help to several other students at the same time?

Some schools, programs, or classes attempt to handle the problem of differing academic abilities by separating students by I.Q. This is particularly true of certain private schools that screen their students with intelligence tests. The idea is that the children as a whole will influence each other and will be able to move together at a faster pace. While this is probably true to some extent, the children are still in lock step and move together. However, some children, due to other abilities: longer attention span, more motivation, special ability to grasp concepts or memorize, etc., learn at different speeds, even to those of similar intellectual ability.

What I consider to be the most important educational objective of all is rarely discussed and almost never successfully implemented below the college level—learning to reason. Instead, elementary and secondary school teachers figure out the answers and spoon feed them to the students, who then memorize them and spit them out when asked to do so. I am not against memorizing. I think it is very important. One must have information to think about. However, the teacher-centered method neglects a very important component—figuring out the answer for oneself before memorizing it. The student then becomes academically dependent on teachers, just as the person who accepts welfare checks becomes economically dependent on the government.

Since acquiring the knowledge, skills and reasoning ability to succeed in life and socializing with twenty-thirty students and a teacher **at the same time** are mutually exclusive goals, parents and students need to decide for themselves which goal is more important to them.

I believe learning to reason is more important than any specific content one learns at any particular time. If students learn to reason, they can teach themselves—any subject, any concept, any time. This is another reason, in addition to added Time on Task and moving at one's own pace according to one's own ability, that the teacher-centered method should be replaced by the learner-centered, self-teaching method. Students are alone. They can think the problem through. Therefore, the most effective number of students for effective learning is one, that is, oneself—no other students, no teacher, just oneself.

Chapter 4
The United States
Educational System

Since humans were first able to communicate, they have been dependent on teachers to teach their children—from tribal elders and storytellers around a campfire to Greek scholars in temples to parents in homes. For parents to become convinced that we need to move away from the teacher-centered method of education to a learner-centered method like TOTIL, they need to understand why teachers were necessary initially and why the method changed to teach large groups of children in classrooms. A short review of the American educational system will help us to understand why this happened in America and other countries as well.

Before discussing the United States educational system, a brief overview of the early educational system of England is warranted. This is the background of most of the colonists who came to America in the 17th and 18th centuries. It was responsible for the system of education and the culture, that is, the philosophy of life and character traits that resulted in it, for most of the American colonists.

In England, during the Middle Ages, most people were illiterate. However, some poor children were taught to read and write by priests and in some towns middle class boys could attend grammar schools where they were taught Latin. Two universities, Oxford and Cambridge, were established in the 13th century. By the 15th century, education had become more common in England and approximately one-third of the population could read and write.[21]

By the 16th century, both boys and girls were being taught to read and write. This was deemed necessary for Bible study, academic scholarship and domestic tasks, including household and estate record-keeping tasks. Upper class women were taught such subjects as classical literature, philosophy, mathematics, astronomy, physics, logic, and rhetoric by their tutors. Middle class women were taught by their mothers.[22]

Many children did not attend school at all and others secured an apprenticeship and learned a trade. Boys who did go to school began grammar school at age seven. Schools began very early in the morning and lasted until 5:00 p.m., six days a week, with few holidays. Teachers were very strict and often beat the children. The brighter students could attend Oxford or Cambridge.[23]

In the mid-16th century, the Humanists insisted on compulsory schooling for all boys and girls in primary and secondary grades, and advanced schooling for boys and qualified women. After King Henry VIII established the Church of England in 1534, he closed the Catholic convent and monastery schools. New Protestant schools opened, funded primarily by members of the new mercantile class.[24]

Protestants who did not belong to the Church of England were not permitted to attend public schools and so attended their own schools.[25] However, most of the teachers of the period were Puritans who were opposed to the Church of England. As a result, Puritan values were disseminated widely. This included the authoritarian family structure with the husband/father as the head of the household and the family household as the center of worship. This replaced the Catholic practice of group worship. Women of all classes were encouraged to become literate enough to read and interpret the Bible for themselves and perhaps to teach it to the children and/or servants of the household."[26] This new sense of individual responsibility would serve the American colonists well in the new world where a strong sense of self-reliance, individualism and independence were necessary for survival.

In colonial America early childhood education was usually provided at home by the mother. This consisted primarily of reading, which used the Bible as text, and a primer or a spelling book. Many children also learned writing and basic arithmetic skills. Once the child had learned to read, the concentration was on learning through private study, that is, Independent Learning. The father would usually contribute to the child's education through vocational training, such as farming. Like today, parents were much too busy to spend a great deal of time as teachers and they believed the children could do it themselves. Beyond the basics, many parents considered book learning frivolous and unimportant to the tasks their children would perform as adults.

Some parents, however, desired more education for their children than could be provided in the home, primarily because of a lack of books, which were very expensive and usually unavailable to individual families. It was decided that a teacher would be hired to read the books and then disseminate the information to groups of children. As a result, the teacher-centered method of education for academic subjects was initiated and the one-room schoolhouse was born, which accommodated students of greatly differing ages and academic abilities.

The teacher would teach a concept to one or a few children at their particular educational level then give them problems and insist that they work them out for themselves and practice while the teacher worked with another set of children. Time on Task would probably have been fairly high compared to today since discipline was very strict and children would not have been interacting much with each other. However, the paucity of books would have limited Time on Task to a significant degree, especially since children would not have been able to take the books home to study.

Some time later, as more and more children entered school, they were assigned to rooms with children of similar ages and educational abilities. This enabled teachers to teach all children at the same time. This was easier and more convenient for the teacher, of course, but, unfortunately, led to more use of the teacher-centered method and less to the learner-centered method whereby the children worked out most of the problems for themselves and learned to think and reason. The teacher-centered method also leads to more student interaction and less Time on Task.

During the colonial period, many schools were specialized as to attendees: gender, race, financial class and various religions. Schools were also specialized as to subjects taught: English, vocations, surveying, navigation, and foreign languages, especially Greek and Latin. Some schools were established and run by private tutors who advertised for students. If they did not perform, they were dismissed.

Attempts at semi-public education in colonial America were primarily the result of Puritan and Congregationalist religious schools in New England. An important objective of education in such schools was, of course, to train children in the tenets of those religions. However, as people of different religions began to immigrate to America, a desire for public schools arose. Thomas Jefferson was the first American leader to propose the idea that the government should be in control of education and that it should be free of religious biases and available to all children regardless of their socio-economic status.[27] Unfortunately, Jefferson appears not to have realized that, if the government controls the schools, they will not be free of political biases.

Private, non-governmental libraries were set up throughout the colonies which were supported by membership fees. These libraries were often used to attain an excellent education through self-teaching/independent learning without attending school. This was different from European libraries which were government supported and controlled so that use was limited to certain privileged people. Once again, with responsibility came authority.

In metropolitan areas of colonial America some schools were started by colonial governments, but they were supported and controlled by the local citizenry. There was extremely little government intervention in education. Elementary education was considered a private, voluntary affair, not the responsibility of any governmental entity. Although Pennsylvania passed a compulsory education law in 1683, it was never strictly enforced.

College attendance was usually restricted to the sons of wealthy land owners or young men who wanted to enter the ministry. Government intervention at the college level was primarily limited to chartering such schools. These schools were then funded and supported by individuals or private groups. Harvard, Princeton and Rutgers were the earliest colonial colleges.

Many of our founding fathers were extremely literate and well educated. An analysis of the educational background of a few of them will help us to understand how they acquired such a superior education.

This knowledge is important to our present discussion of teacher-centered vs. learner-centered education.

Benjamin Franklin, the youngest of fifteen children in his family, started grammar school at age eight and left at age ten due to his father's death and his need to support himself. He was completely self-taught after age ten. At age thirteen, Franklin became a printer's apprentice to his brother. Later, he became an author, diplomat, philosopher, scientist and one of America's greatest statesmen. He was a self-educated, self-made man who succeeded primarily because of personal characteristics of self-reliance, perseverance and independence.[28]

George Washington was one of eight children. George was the oldest of Augustine Washington and Mary Ball Washington's six children. He had two older half brothers from his father's first marriage. His early education consisted of reading, writing and basic arithmetic. George's father died when George was only eleven years old. His two older half brothers inherited most of the estate and, even though George was a gentleman, he did not learn Latin, Greek or any other foreign language, nor did he go to England to finish his education, as had his two half brothers. George excelled in mathematics and learned surveying. Although his formal education ended at age fifteen, he read voraciously and studied independently for the rest of his life. He was appointed Commander-in-Chief of the entire United States military in 1775 by the Second Continental Congress, and became the first President of the United States in 1789.[29]

John Adams learned to read, write and perform basic mathematics at home. Then, he began his formal education in a common school in Braintree, now Quincy, Massachusetts. He earned a scholarship to Harvard, graduated at age twenty and became a lawyer. He was a signer of the Declaration of Independence from the state of Massachusetts in 1776 and became the second President of the United States in 1796.[30]

Thomas Jefferson was tutored by Reverend James Maury. At age nine he began to study Latin, Greek and French. At age sixteen, Jefferson attended William and Mary College in Williamsburg, Virginia. He became a lawyer, agronomist, musician, scientist, philosopher, author, architect, inventor and statesman. Of course, he is best known as the third President of the United States and the author of the Declaration of Independence.[31]

When America declared its independence in 1776, school attendance was voluntary and educational institutions were competitive. Those that were ineffective went out of business. Those that survived produced students who were very literate and able to read and understand complex writings, such as the Federalist Papers. Education was relatively inexpensive and for those who could not afford to pay, education was provided free.

Public education was discussed during the Constitutional Convention and it was agreed that education was a private matter and that the government, especially the federal government, should not be involved in it. Because our founding fathers had been mostly self-educated, they supported local educational institutions, if any.[32]

This philosophy of non-governmental intervention in education did not last much longer. By the end of the 19th century, free public elementary school education was available to all students, and by 1918 all states had passed compulsory school attendance laws for elementary school children. In the 20th century most states raised the age of compulsory school attendance to sixteen.

Prior to the 20th century, it was common for examinations to be given at the end of the eighth grade which determined which advanced track students would follow, or if they would be dropped from school. Most students left school and entered the work force or raised families. Some school districts, mostly in foreign countries, offered technical school education after the eighth grade which prepared students for skilled trades or other specific job training, including apprenticeships. Approximately five percent of students were allowed to continue to high school which was often preparation for college. Only about six percent of students graduated from high school prior to 1900. This increased to eighty-five percent by 1996.

In the late 19th century, concurrent with the rise of compulsory public school education, a new, soon to be very influential, movement in education began. This was called "progressive education." This is the belief that education must be based on the principle that humans are social animals who learn best through real-life activities with other people in a learn-by-doing, hands-on approach. According to this philosophy, the primary goal of education is socialization, not education, that is, knowledge or job training. Progressive education was, in large part, a protest against competitive meritocracy and vocational preparation for workers in a capitalistic society. George Counts, the leader of a politically-oriented group of progressive educators dared schools to "build a new social order" in *The Social Frontier*.[33]

The most famous early practitioner of progressive education was Francis Parker. In 1875 Parker became Superintendent of Schools in Quincy, Massachusetts and replaced the traditional books for reading, spelling, and grammar with the children's own writings and teacher-prepared materials.[34]

The best-known proponent of progressive education was John Dewey. In 1899, Dewey published a book called *School and Society* and progressive education began its meteoric rise. Dewey is considered the father of the movement which became popular in the 1920's and 1930's. This is the same time that the socialist political movement in America changed its name to the progressive movement because socialism had become unpopular.

Dewey also greatly influenced constructivist learning theory. Constructivism adopted most of Dewey's ideas, primarily that learning is a social process with much interaction between teacher and students and that children learn by doing in a hands-on approach, that is, from their own experiences.

In 1919, the Progressive Education Association, which aimed at "reforming the entire school system of America," was founded. Parker and Dewey's followers decided that secondary education was too elitist and needed to be restructured and democratized to better attain the goals of progressive education. Thus, the American Comprehensive High School was born. This supposedly maximized the changing and more technological needs of businesses rather than specific training/apprenticeships. It was a one-size-fits-all approach. All students followed essentially the same curriculum which was primarily preparation for college.

This change toward progressive education involved allowing entrance and a free education to all students in the district. No entrance examination was given and academic standards were greatly relaxed. A very important goal of American secondary education now was to minimize the number of students who dropped out of school prior to attaining a high school diploma.[35] The purported reason for keeping students in school was that students would be more economically successful with a diploma. Some people, however, believed that at least part of the motivation was for the school systems to obtain more money from the government and/or more control over students and their parents.

Christopher Koliba, Ph.D., a follower of John Dewey and a prolific writer of articles in favor of progressive education, discussed the conflict among three different aims of education: education to prepare students for employment; education to provide basic academic skills and knowledge; and education to socialize students to prepare them to function well in a democratic society. While many people, including Koliba, believe that all three goals should be considered, I wish to emphasize that these goals are, for the most part, mutually exclusive. One goal is teacher centered, group oriented and politically motivated. The other two goals are learner centered, individual oriented and academically motivated. Relative to the primary goal of the proponents of progressive education, Koliba quoted another researcher and strong proponent of progressive education, L. H. Ehman (1980, 113), as follows:

> The findings from this review suggest that the manifest curriculum (i.e. direct instruction involving courses and texts in civics, government, and other social studies courses) is not as important as the latent curriculum in influencing political attitudes. This latent curriculum includes how classes are taught [in a group, by a teacher], not the subject matter itself. This classroom climate is directly manipulable by teachers and represents a potentially important level in the political education of youth. The entire school governance climate, which is another aspect of the latent curriculum, is another correlate of student political attitudes.[36]

Ehman is very explicit that, to attain the primary goal of progressive education, which is to influence political attitudes, it is not necessary or advisable to depend on the content of textbooks or courses. Rather, it is best to accomplish this goal by following the primary mantra of progressive education which is a group-oriented, "hands on" approach led by a teacher. This accustoms students to think as a group and act as a group. This method significantly reduces the academic content, the amount of knowledge gained or skills taught, and subordinates it to the socio-political content, that is, learning to work and think as a group. It should be clear that, for the proponents of progressive education, the American educational system is not a failure. For the most part, it is accomplishing what they intend for it to accomplish.

Progressive education is still the ruling educational philosophy in America today. In 1957, after the success of Sputnik, a Russian space satellite, some educators and politicians began to rethink progressive educational theory. They realized that students from most other countries were superior to students in the United States in many academic subjects and technical skills, but especially, and most importantly, in mathematics and science. However, this skepticism did not last long and progressive education continues to be the dominant educational philosophy.

With the arrival of progressive education, schools were once again seen as the primary instrument to promote the philosophies of a particular group. But now, it was no longer the religious philosophy of the parents and surrounding community that was being promoted, as had been the case in colonial America and many other countries and times, nor the philosophy of the upper classes as had been the case in ancient Greece, Rome and other countries. Now it was the political philosophy of influential educators and members of the federal government, who were becoming more and more politically progressive, that is, socialistic, that was being promoted.

I have attempted to keep politics out of a discussion on how to improve education because it is such a divisive issue. Unfortunately, this is not possible. Politics is inextricably linked to our educational system, especially since the late 19th century when the political progressive movement began promoting progressive education in America in order to attain its political goals as has been explicitly stated above by proponents of the system. Progressive education is a direct outgrowth of the progressive political movement and cannot be separated from it.

In progressive education, as in the socialist/progressive system of government, it is the group that matters, not the individual. That is one reason that most public money for education is spent on raising the educational level of mediocre and poor students, rather than academically superior students. This is true not only in America, but in most other countries. An individual is not really important except as he or she contributes to the group, and humility and dependence on others are virtues, primarily because they make people easier to control. Independence, self- confidence, self-sufficiency and personal responsibility are considered vices because they make people more difficult to control. Prior to the introduction of progressivism, especially in colonial America, Canada and many other countries, the opposite was true. Independence, self-reliance, personal responsibility and self-confidence were virtues. If we expect to improve our children's education, we need to rediscover these lost values.

Chapter 5
PISA Rankings of Countries
on Education in 2009

Every three years, the Organization for Economic Co-operation and Development (OECD) conducts its *Programme for International Student Assessment* (PISA) tests which assess the reading, math and science skills of fifteen-year-old students in numerous countries and ranks them. Tests were given in 2000, 2003, 2006 and 2009. Each year focuses on a separate subject; however, all three subjects are tested.[37] Table 2 presents the results of these tests from 2009. Table 3 presents the results of the subjects that were the focus of the study for 2000,2003 and 2006.

In the 2009 PISA tests, with sixty-five countries competing, students from Chinese, or Chinese-dominated, countries were clearly superior to students from other countries. Students from Shanghai, China finished first in all subjects—math, reading and science. Students from Hong Kong, China finished third in math and science. Singapore ranked second in math and fourth in science. The only non-ethnic Chinese dominated countries that ranked in the upper five countries were South Korea (second in reading and fourth in math), Japan (fifth in reading) and Finland (second in sciences and third in reading). As can be seen from Table 3, the only non-Asian country that scored in the top five countries was Finland, which had been the top scorer in previous years when the only Asian countries competing were South Korea and Japan because they were the only Asian countries that belonged to OECD.[39]

Table 2: PISA Rankings of Countries in 2009

<u>Math</u>	<u>Sciences</u>	<u>Reading</u>
1. Shanghai, China 603	Shanghai, China 575	Shanghai, China 556
2. Singapore 562	Finland 554	South Korea 539
3. Hong Kong, Ch 555	Hong Kong, Ch. 549	Finland 536
4. South Korea 546	Singapore 542	Hong Kong, Ch 533
5. Taiwan 543	Japan 539	Singapore 526
6. Finland 541	South Korea 638	Canada 524
7. Liechtenstein 536	New Zealand 532	New Zealand 521
8. Switzerland 534	Canada 529	Japan 520
9. Japan 529	Estonia 528	Australia 515
10. Canada 527	Australia 527	Netherlands 508
11. Netherlands 526	Netherlands 522	Belgium 506
12. Macau, China 525	Liechtenstein 520	Norway 503
13. New Zealand 519	Germany 520	Estonia 501
14. Belgium 515	Taiwan 520	Switzerland 501
15. Australia 514	Switzerland 517	Poland 500
16. Germany 513	United Kingdom 514	Iceland 500
17. Estonia 512	Slovenia 512	**United States 500**
18. Iceland 507	Macau, China 511	Liechtenstein 499
19. Denmark 503	Poland 508	Sweden 497
20. Slovenia 501	Ireland 508	Germany 497
21. Norway 498	Belgium 507	Ireland 496
22. France 497	Hungary 503	France 496
23. Slovakia 497	**United States** 502	Taiwan 495
24. Austria 496	Norway 500	Denmark 495
25. Poland 495	Czech Republic 500	United Kingdom 494
26. Sweden 494	Denmark 499	Hungary 494
27. Czech Republic 493	France 498	Portugal 489
28. United Kingdom 492	Iceland 496	Macau, China 487
29. Hungary 490	Sweden 495	Italy 486
30. **United States** 487	Latvia 494	Latvia 484
65. Kyrgyzstan 331	Kyrgyzstan 330	Kyrgyzstan 314[38]

Table 3: PISA Rankings of Countries

2000	2003	2006
Reading	**Math**	**Sciences**
1. Finland 546	1. Finland 544	1. Finland 563
2. Canada 534	2. South Korea 542	2. Canada 534
3. New Zealand 529	3. Netherlands 538	3. Japan 531
4. Australia 528	4. Japan 534	4. New Zealand 530
5. Ireland 527	5. Canada 532	5. Australia 527
6. South Korea 525	6. Belgium 529	6. Netherlands 525
7. United Kingdom 523	7. Switzerland 527	7. S. Korea 522
8. Japan 522	8. Australia 524	8. Germany 516
9. Sweden 516	9. New Zealand 523	9. U. Kingdom 515
10. Austria 507	10. Czech Republic 516	10. Czech Rep. 513
11. Belgium 507	11. Iceland 515	11. Switzerland 512
12. Iceland 507	12. Denmark 514	12. Austria 511
13. Norway 505	13. France 511	13. Belgium 510
14. France 505	14. Sweden 503	14. Ireland 508
15. U.S.A. 504	15. Austria 506	15. Hungary 504
16. Denmark 497	16. Germany 503	16. Sweden 503
17. Switzerland 494	17. Ireland 503	17. Poland 498
18. Spain 493	18. Slovakia 498	18. Denmark 496
19. Czech Rep 492	19. Norway 495	19. France 495
20. Italy 487	20. Luxembourg 493	20. Iceland 491
21. Germany 484	21. Poland 490	**21. U.S.A. 489**
22. Hungary 480	22. Hungary 490	22. Slovakia 488
23. Poland 479	23. Spain 485	23. Spain 488
24. Greece 474	**24. U.S.A. 483**	24. Norway 487
25. Portugal 470	25. Italy 466	25. Luxembourg 486
26. Luxembourg 441	26. Portugal 466	26. Italy 475
27. Mexico 422	27. Greece 445	27. Portugal 474
28. Turkey 423	28. Greece 473	
29. Mexico 385	29. Turkey 424	
30. Mexico 410[40]		

I will examine the educational systems of the five highest-scoring PISA countries in the 2009 study to determine which factors might best account for the difference in achievement between students in these countries and lower-ranking students from the United States. I am using the 2009 PISA scores because they are the most recent scores and because many more countries were included than in the previous years the PISA tests were given: 2000, 2003 and 2006. I am also including an overview of the educational system of Canada because their educational background and culture are very similar to the United States, yet their students performed much better in all PISA tests. Canada ranked tenth in math, eighth in science and sixth in reading, while the United States ranked thirtieth in math, twenty-third in science and seventeenth in reading out of sixty-five countries tested.

Shanghai, China

As stated above, Shanghai, China ranked first out of sixty-five countries in the 2009 PISA tests for math, science, and reading.[41] Shanghai was not represented in the PISA tests in 2000, 2003 or 2006. The OECD, which supervises the PISA tests, examined rural areas and very poor areas of China and found that the rural areas matched Shanghai's quality and some of the poorer areas performed close to the OECD average. This indicates that educational excellence in China is not restricted to the populous Chinese cities.

Prior to 1949, education in China had concentrated primarily on educating the elite. Most workers, peasants and females were uneducated or undereducated. Approximately eighty percent of the population was illiterate. In 1949, when Mao Zedong assumed leadership over the People's Republic of China, he stressed the superiority of workers and peasants and their "hand skill." With the Cultural Revolution and the nationalization of education in 1966-1976, prejudice against knowledge and education was encouraged by the government. Books, and buildings were destroyed and teachers were persecuted. Admittance to higher education was now based on recommendation, not examination, primarily of children of Communist Party officials by minor officials in towns and cities trying to curry favor with their political bosses. The quality of education declined, of course, and China's need for competent workers in an increasingly scientific and technological society was not met.[42]

In the 1980's, primarily under the leadership of Deng Xiaoping, China decided it needed to make great advances in science and technology and a push for modernization began. Government control of education was relaxed somewhat, although the political system remained very socialistic. University examinations were reintroduced, and admittance was, once again, approved on the basis of academic excellence. Successful applicants received scholarships "Political activism was no longer regarded as an important measure of individual performance, and even the development of commonly approved political attitudes and political background was secondary to achievement. This policy contrasted with the previous one, which touted increased enrollments for egalitarian reasons."[43] Deng Xiaoping also encouraged the improvement and expansion of education at lower levels, that is, primary school and secondary school. Considerable autonomy was permitted among regions, provinces, and special municipalities, although central authority in the Ministry of Education was still maintained until 1985 when the responsibility for education in China was given to the Central Committee of the Chinese Communist Party and implemented by local governments.[44]

In 1986, a compulsory education law took effect in China which mandated nine years of education for all children. To help assure adherence to this law, employers were forbidden to hire young people who had not finished their nine years of compulsory education. This law also divided China educationally into three categories: cities and other developed areas; towns and villages with medium development; and economically backward areas.

Subjects taught at the primary school level were: Chinese, mathematics, physical education, music, drawing, history, geography and moral training, which stressed love of country, love of the party and love of people. A foreign language, usually English, was added, usually about third grade. Courses on morality and ethics were required. Chinese and mathematics accounted for about sixty percent of the curriculum.

Education in China has been a see-saw affair because leaders could not decide whether to stress ideology or professional and technical competence. Unfortunately, these goals have proven to be incompatible in China, as they have in other countries throughout history.[45]

Academic subjects taught during secondary school in China include: Chinese, mathematics, English, physics, chemistry, biology, geography, history, politics, music, fine arts, physical education, technology, and computing. Vocational subjects are taught at some schools. Chinese, mathematics and English are considered the most important subjects as they will be required in the Gaokao exam.[46] This exam is required for entrance into colleges and universities and is the equivalent of the American SAT and ACT college entrance exams. However, the *Gaokao* is considered much more difficult and is about a third longer. In June 2010, the first day of the exams, three Chinese students who were about to take the test died: one committed suicide by jumping from a twelve-story hospital building; another hanged himself four hours before the exam; and the cause of death for the third student was unknown at the time the article was written.[47]

Education in China usually begins with preschool between ages three and six. Primary school is for children between ages 6-12 (Grades K-5) ; junior secondary school accommodates ages twelve-fifteen (Grades 6-9); senior secondary school accommodates ages fifteen-eighteen (Grades 10-12); and vocational secondary school accommodates ages 15-18, (Grades 10-12).[48]

Since 1997, the school schedule in China has been five days a week for nine and one half months with a summer vacation in July and August and a winter vacation in January and February. In rural areas school days are shorter. However, urban [Shanghai] and key (academically elite) schools almost always function on a six day, year-round schedule to prepare students to pass exams to acquire further education and high-level jobs.[49] Time on Task.

Singapore

In the PISA rankings for 2009 Singapore ranked second in math, fourth in science and fifth in reading out of sixty-five countries. It was not represented in the PISA tests in 2000, 2003 or 2006.[50] In 2010, the British Education Minister selected Singapore's education system for commendation.

Education in Singapore is managed by the Ministry of Education (MOE) which controls state schools and supervises private schools. Home-schooling and religious institutions are permitted. Education in Singapore is highly valued and rigorous, and is based on a meritocracy system determined by examinations. In 1987, English was designated as the main language of instruction. The 2000 Compulsory Education Act mandated education for children of primary school age, that is, ages seven through twelve.[51]

While pre-school training is not compulsory, most children do attend some kind of private, pre-school facility from ages two through six. This includes nursery school, Kindergarten 1 and Kindergarten 2.[52]

Primary school education, which is mandatory, begins at age seven and lasts for six years. Subjects taught at this level include: English, Mother Tongue (Chinese, Malay, Tamil or a non-Tamil Indian Language) and math. Science teaching begins at Primary 3. Mandarin is strongly encouraged as the Chinese language to be selected to encourage uniformity. Several other, less academic subjects are also included. At the end of primary school a student must take the all-important *Primary School Leaving Examination*.[53]

Students in secondary school are tracked/streamed according to their PSLE tests into one of the four-year tracks: Special, Express, Normal Academic or Normal Technical. The Special and Express tracks lead to the *Singapore-Cambridge GCE O'Level* examination. The Normal Track leads to a N-level examination with the possibility of a fifth year followed by an O-level examination. However, as of 2004, selected students in the Normal Track have been permitted to take the O-level exam without first taking the N-level exam. Compulsory subjects for a GCE 'O' level candidate are: English, Mother Tongue, mathematics, combined humanities, science and one other subject.[54]

In 2007, the Integrated Programme was introduced. The IP program allows gifted students, usually the top students from the Special and Express tracks, to bypass the "O" levels examination at the end of four years and go directly into junior colleges. These students will then take the "A" levels examination, International Baccalaureate or equivalent examination immediately after six years of secondary education at the age of 18. Students in the IP program are expected to be independent learners.[55]

In Singapore the school year consists of four terms of ten weeks each. Twelve weeks of vacation are allowed.[56] Lessons in Mother Tongue (Chinese, Malay, Tamil or a non-Tamil Indian language) are conducted in school after regular school hours.[57]

A study of three hundred forty Singaporean children was conducted to determine children's views on school. The following excerpt from a paper by Lay See Yeo and Christine Clarke of the National Institute of Education at Nanyang Technological University in Singapore reveals some of the results of that study.

> Perhaps what set the Singaporean children apart from their counterparts in other countries was their highly school-and work-centered view of life, although they also enjoyed school (Sharpe, 2002). When asked about life outside of school, the young children in the Sharpe (2002) study mostly reported watching television, with the remainder of the time taken up by tuition [instruction]. The Singaporean children's serious view of school was reflected in their limited range of social experiences, concern with tests and examinations, and the need to please parents by earning high grades (Sharpe, 1002).[58] Time on Task.

Hong Kong, China

Hong Kong ranked third in math and science and fourth in reading out of sixty-five countries in the PISA tests in 2009. It was not represented in the PISA tests in 2000, 2003 or 2006.[59]

There is evidence that some form of education has existed in Hong Kong since before 200 A.D. Such institutions taught reading, writing and vocational subjects. Later, the emphasis was placed on preparation for the civil service examination. One of the earliest schools was Li Ying College established in 1075. After the British arrived in 1841, education was provided primarily by Protestant and Catholic missionaries. In 1961 the British modernized the educational system of Hong Kong. A revision was instituted in 1971. The present system has been in place since 2007.[60]

The first three years of education in Hong Kong is called Kindergarten. This is followed by six years of primary education and three years of secondary education. All of these levels are compulsory. Because the demand for classes is so great, many schools split the school day into A.M. and P.M. sessions. The school year extends from September to June for Kindergarten students and September to July for primary and secondary school students.[61]

Compared to other educational systems throughout the world, the Hong Kong system is extremely competitive. The current workload of a primary student in Hong Kong includes approximately three to four hours of homework every night and "cram" schools are very popular. The curriculum concentrates on quantity, memorization, and the acquisition of certificates, rather than decision-making ability. Although most Hong Kong parents are proud of the superior grades their children make in international tests, most who can afford it send their children to overseas schools.[62]

Discipline is extremely strict in Hong Kong schools, which have a demerit system for even very minor infractions. Three minor infractions constitute a major infraction. Three major infractions merit automatic suspension or expulsion if the child is over the compulsory education age. These demerits carry a great deal of weight and can be put on a student's report card. This may affect their career opportunities.[63]

Children are ranked very early in their career. After three years of Kindergarten, in Primary 4 (equivalent of about third grade in the U.S.), children are required to choose between tracts: Science, Arts and Commerce. At the end of Primary 5, the student takes the *Hong Kong Certificate of Education Examination* (HKCEE). If the student passes this exam, s/he is promoted to Form 6 (equivalent of fifth grade in the U.S.) The next examination is the *Hong Kong Advanced Level Examination* (HKALE), which is considered the university entrance examination. At this point, tracking becomes even more rigid, dividing students into the Mathematics/Engineering Tract, the Biology/Medical Tract or the Arts Tract.[64] The extended school hours and study hours, as well as the strict discipline of Hong Kong schools, result in a high level of Time on Task.

South Korea

South Korea ranked fourth in math, sixth in science and second in reading out of sixty-five countries in the PISA tests in 2009. It ranked sixth out of twenty-seven countries in reading in the PISA tests in 2000; second out of twenty-nine countries in math in the PISA tests in 2003; and seventh out of thirty countries in science in the PISA tests in 2006.[65]

Formal education has always been respected in Korea. The National Confucian Academy was founded and operated by the state in 372. Another institution of higher learning, The National Confucian College, was founded in 682. Also, in 992, National University was established in Kaesong. Education in Korea at this time was greatly influenced by China and consisted primarily of studying the Confucian classics. Primary education was taught in private schools and there were two kinds of secondary education: one in the villages and another in Hangyang (present-day Seoul). After the introduction of the Chinese civil service exam in the mid-10th century, education was directed toward preparing young aristocratic males for public service. This system of education survived until the 19th century.[66]

Education in South Korea is controlled by the Ministry of Education, Science and Technology. However, education in Kindergarten is not publicly administered. Children may enter Kindergarten as early as age three. They are grouped with other children whose ages range from three to six or seven. Then, the child enters a public or a private elementary school, which continues to the sixth grade. Advancement is determined solely by age from Kindergarten to high school. The private elementary schools are similar to public elementary schools in curriculum and are extremely expensive.[67]

In middle school, students begin classes with a thirty-minute block of time, followed by seven forty-five-minute lessons. Students attend school from Monday through Friday and on some Saturdays (about one half). Their vacations consist of five weeks in the summer, one month at Christmas and two weeks in spring.[68]

Middle school attendance is mandatory but high school is not. Middle schools include Grades 7-9. At the end of middle school, students must take an examination to determine which high school they may attend, or if they will attend a vocational or technical school. This is different from the pre-1980's when children were assigned to schools according to their academic ability.[69]

Many middle school students attend after school academies called *hagwon* to prepare for examinations. Many parents consider these *hagwon* studies more important than the child's regular school. As a result of the need to prepare for these high school entrance examinations, many middle school students stay at school until midnight. Many high school students also stay at school until midnight for intensive self-study sessions.[70] Time on Task—about fifteen hours each week day.

High schools include students from Grades 10-12, ages twelve-thirteen and fifteen-sixteen. Some high schools specialize in particular subjects such as science, foreign languages and art. According to an OECD (Organization for Economic Cooperation and Development) report, ninety-seven percent of adults in South Korea complete high school, although high school attendance is not mandatory.[71]

Vocational high schools specialize in areas such as technology, agriculture or finance. Attending a vocational high school does not preclude a student from later attending a college or university. Admission to vocational college or polytechnic schools is the same as it is for academic schools—the *Korean College Scholastic Ability Test.*[72]

The *KCSA* is considered an extremely difficult test and can be taken only once a year. Many students begin studying for this test in Kindergarten. Students usually sacrifice family life and social life to get into the best university possible and entire communities cooperate. "Examinations are very serious times of the year and they change the whole pattern of society. Businesses often start at 10.00 a.m. to accommodate parents who have helped their children study late into the night, and on the evenings before exams, recreational facilities, such as tennis clubs, close early to facilitate study for these exams."[73] Time on Task.

Some critics of the South Korean educational system have pointed out that children sacrifice their childhood and that there are numerous suicides due to anxiety from the continual pressure of tests. They also point out that this system is a teacher-centered approach, where information is primarily one way, from teacher to student, and will not change to a learner-centered approach, which is more important for success in post-secondary education and in life, without major obstacles.[74]

Taiwan

Taiwan ranked fifth in math, fourteenth in science and twenty-third in reading out of sixty-five countries in the PISA tests in 2009. [75] It was not represented in the PISA tests for 2000, 2003 or 2006.

At age four, children in Taiwan begin a two-year preschool program. Private preschools outnumber public preschools by a ratio of two to one. After preschool, children finish six years of elementary education followed by three years of junior high school, both of which are compulsory. Most teachers teach the same students from Grade 7 through Grade 9. To continue on to senior secondary school, students must take national exams to determine if they will be placed in a program with three years of high school, three years of vocational school or five years of junior college.[76]

Preparing for the national exam, taken after junior high school, creates a great deal of anxiety. For Taiwanese students, secondary school is one of the most difficult periods of their lives. The school day extends from 7:30 a.m. to 5:30 p.m. The school year consists of two hundred days compared to one hundred days in the United States. School begins with a forty-five-minute or one hour study period. The more difficult classes, such as math, Chinese literature, science and English, are taken in the morning when, it is believed, the students will have clearer minds that will enable them to concentrate better. A forty-minute nap is then taken to refresh them. Some students choose to study during this period. Some students receive extra instruction for which they must pay the equivalent of eighty-five dollars U.S. per subject.[77]

Students and parents believe that effort, not ability, is the most important determinant of academic success. Competition is very strong. It has been called "academic Darwinism." Discipline is stricter in Taiwanese schools, where teachers are more effective in classroom management, than in American schools. Parents are very supportive of the rigorous academic training and discipline of Taiwanese students.[78] Many students take extra classes after school. The most popular of these classes are in "cram" schools. These private schools are geared to preparing students for the examinations. Throughout the school day and week more time is spent in academically oriented activities than in socially oriented activities.[79] Time on Task.

Japan

Japan ranked fifth in science, ninth in math and eighth in reading out of sixty-five countries in the PISA tests in 2009. It also ranked eighth in reading out of twenty-seven countries in the PISA tests in 2000; fourth out of twenty-nine countries in math in the PISA tests in 2003; and third in science out of thirty countries in the PISA tests in 2006.[80]

Japanese education began in the sixth century when the Chinese system of education was introduced to Japan from China along with Buddhism, Confucianism and the Chinese system of writing and literature. By the ninth century, present-day Kyoto, the capital of Japan at the time, had five institutions of higher learning. In the Medieval Period, education was primarily the responsibility of the Buddhist monasteries and, in the fifteenth century, the Ashikaga School flourished as a center of higher learning. In the 16th century, Japan began to interact with Europe and Christian religious schools were opened, which taught Japanese, Latin and western classical music. However, by 1640, all foreigners had been ordered out of Japan and virtually all foreign contact was banned for 200 years.[81]

In 1600 few people of lower economic status in Japan could read or write. By 1867 learning had become widespread and the literacy rate was over 80 percent for men and about 70 percent for women. It was even higher in cities like Edo and Osaka. Education of the lower classes was generally restricted to the basics, that is, reading, writing, and arithmetic. Emphasis was placed on learning calligraphy and use of the abacus. However, some poorer students were accepted into private academies along with Samurai to study military subjects and European studies, including Western medicine.[82]

After 1868, leaders in Japan became interested in becoming more modern to catch up with the West in many areas, including education. Groups were sent abroad to study the educational systems of leading western countries, including the United States. They returned with ideas about the hierarchy and organization of these educational systems. Although many western ideas were adopted, many were modified to meet the more conservative and traditional orientation of the Japanese culture.[83]

In the early 20th century, public education in Japan was available to all children at the primary level, but at higher levels it was elitist and sexist. However, Christian missionaries opened schools and expanded educational opportunities for women at the secondary level and founded some universities. German influences were quite noticeable in the universities.[84]

By the end of World War II, education in Japan was in shambles. Because of the defeat, many Japanese were disenchanted with previous ideas, including those related to education. With the occupation of Japan by the United States in 1945, many new ideas about education were implemented. These were aimed at eliminating the elitism of the pre-war Japanese educational system. Three levels of schooling prior to university education were implemented: elementary school for Grades 1-6; middle school for Grades 7-9; and high school for Grades 10-12.[85]

Compulsory education for all was extended to cover education through middle school. Curricula and textbooks were also revised and the nationalistic morals course was abolished and replaced with social studies. This allowed indoctrination in a more acceptable United States-oriented philosophy rather than the Japanese and German-oriented philosophy that had been taught previously. Teachers' unions were also established at this time.[86]

After Japan regained full national sovereignty in 1952, it began to reject some of the American ideas and to modify some of the changes it had made in education and educational administration to incorporate Japanese ideas. However, because of the democratic ideas that had been adopted, and the establishment of teachers' unions during the American occupation, strong disagreement developed among the government, teachers and students, and there were numerous student strikes.[87]

Japanese children are first taught verbal skills, social skills and quantitative skills at home. There are many television programs geared toward helping to educate these children. Most children then enter a public or private preschool or day-care center. These institutions enroll over ninety percent of all children before their entrance into first grade.[88]

Japanese elementary schools begin at 8:30 a.m. and end at 3:00 p.m. Middle and secondary schools begin at 8:30 a.m. and usually end at 5:00 p.m. with a half day on Saturdays. From 3:00 p.m. to 5:00 p.m. students attend compulsory clubs and other extracurricular activities, including physical activities.[89]

The Japanese school year lasts from April 1st to March 31st in a trimester system. The Japanese believe that academic progress is due to effort and not ability. Teaching is primarily through lecturing and the main goal is to cover the material in the very demanding curriculum. Children are expected to behave. School authorities also have the authority to regulate the behavior of students outside the school setting. Three problems are of primary concern to school authorities: bullying, which is excessive; drop-out rates; and accommodation of children who have been out of the country for an extended length of time and are not prepared for the rigors of the Japanese school system, either academically or behaviorally.[90]

Approximately 30 percent of students in upper secondary schools, Grades 10-12, are enrolled in technical and vocational courses, rather than the general academic program. The large majority of these students are enrolled in business and industrial courses, although courses in information processing, navigation, fish farming and ceramics are also offered.[91]

Some critics of the Japanese educational system believe that many of the social problems of young people in Japan today are a result of the excessive demands of the educational system, which lead to great anxiety in the students and excessive numbers of suicides.

Over 50 percent of all children in elementary and middle schools attend special private schools called *"juku"* after school and on weekends to help them prepare for the all-important examinations or to help them keep up with regular schoolwork. These schools are reasonably priced and most parents can afford them.[92] Time on Task.

Finland

Finland placed second in science and reading and sixth in math out of sixty-five countries in the PISA tests in 2009. It also placed first in reading out of twenty-seven countries in the PISA tests in 2000; and first in math out of twenty-nine countries in the PISA tests in

2003.[93] Finland's students scored highest in the world in science and reading and second in math out of thirty countries in the PISA exams in 2006.[94]

Finland's reputation for excellence in education is relatively recent. In the 1960's Finland was considered to have a poor educational system and numerous students left the public school system in favor of private schools. Citizens and public officials decided to concentrate on revising the system and, as is obvious, were very successful. Presently, there are very few private schools in Finland, probably both because of the dramatic increase in the quality of the public schools and because of the oppressive rules imposed on private schools by the government, which strictly regulates such schools.[95]

Education in Finland is based on a nine-year comprehensive school system. School begins at age seven and is compulsory until the age of fifteen or sixteen.[96] Students remain with the same teacher for many years in elementary school. Since primary and secondary schooling is combined, students do not change schools after primary school. At the end of primary school a student chooses between a vocational school and an academically-oriented curriculum.[97]

Children begin studying algebra, geometry and statistics in the first grade.[98] An additional teacher is present in each classroom to help students who are struggling with a particular lesson or subject. Such students are not separated from their own age group regardless of their ability.[99] Students who have problems learning on an ongoing basis are assigned tutors and remedial specialists from the first day they are evaluated until the day they graduate.[100]

One of the criticisms of Finland's educational system is that, although a great deal of time is spent on assisting children who have learning difficulties, little time is spent on children who are very gifted. Finland's Education Minister, Henna Virkkunen, agrees with this criticism and has started a pilot project to support students who are gifted in certain areas.[101]

The OECD states that pupils in Finland's schools have the fewest class hours in the developed world.[102] Yet, Finnish students perform better on the PISA tests than all other countries, except Asian countries whose students devote over sixty hours a week on "schooling." Why? To discover the answer to this mystery, numerous educators from around the world have studied Finland's educational system and many of them, including a representative from the United States, have even visited Finland. Most of them still do not have an answer to the question. I am presenting explanations of some who purport to have an answer below.

According to Ellen Gamerman, "One explanation for the Finn's success [in education] is their love of reading. Parents of newborns receive a government-paid gift pack that includes a picture book. Some libraries are attached to shopping malls, and a book bus travels to more remote neighborhoods like a Good Humor truck."[103]

Some educators believe that the low level of immigration into Finland is an advantage for Finland's educational system since most children who enter first grade speak Finnish as their native language.[104]

Taksin Nuoret, after considerable study, concluded that the Finnish language plays an important part in Finnish students' extraordinary educational success. Nuoret concludes that transparent spelling, rich derivational morphology, and transparent morphology combine to give Finnish students an advantage over other students.[105]

According to Hannu Simola, Ph.D., a professor on the Faculty of Behavioral Sciences at the University of Helsinki, Finland's students belong to a culture that believes that effort is extremely important for success in a small border nation, like Singapore and Taiwan.[106]

An analysis of the Finnish educational system leads me to the conclusion that, as in other academically-successful countries, extended Time on Task, especially within the classroom in this case, explains this success. As Ellen Gamerman of Helsinki, Finland states, "Early on, kids do a lot without adults hovering."[107] This suggests that students are utilizing a modified self-teaching approach. This is possible, in part because, as has already been suggested above by Hannu Simola, Finnish students belong to a culture that believes in effort and discipline.

Also, because students who are having difficulty with a lesson are temporarily separated from the group (perhaps even in the same room) by the additional teacher, tutor or remedial teacher for extra instruction, they are working without distractions—and they probably finish this work at home, which leads to even more studying.

In addition, the faster students can continue with their lessons without having to wait for the slower students to catch up, or for the teacher to explain the lesson again. Also, the fact that reading is a national pastime, as suggested above, means that, although assigned lessons for homework are at a minimum, it is likely that much studying gets accomplished away from the classroom. Once again, additional Time on Task (not schooling) leads to academic success.

Canada

Canada placed eighth in science, sixth in reading and tenth in math out of sixty-five countries in the PISA tests in 2009. Canada also ranked second in reading out of twenty-seven countries in the PISA tests in 2000; fifth in math out of twenty-nine countries in the PISA tests in 2003; and second in science out of thirty countries in the PISA tests in 2006.[108]

In the 17th century, education in the rural areas of French Canada was conducted primarily by family members. This education was primarily in the skills needed for survival. Young males were involved in apprenticeships. However, sometimes family members also taught reading and writing to their children in addition to the Catholic religion. In the towns, formal elementary education was provided in catechism, reading, writing and arithmetic and was provided by Catholic priests. Educating native Canadians in the Catholic religion and Catholic customs was the primary goal.[109]

After the British won Canada from the French in the Conquest of 1759-60, the British were concerned with the large contingent of hostile French citizenry. The main focus of education became the drive to promote identification with Protestantism, instead of Catholicism; the English language, instead of the French language; and British customs, instead of French customs. These attempts had limited success as they were vigorously fought by the Catholic Church and members of the local communities. Education continued to be more the responsibility of the home rather than classrooms.[110]

The rise of interest in formal education for the masses in British Canada in the 19th century was not the result of the desire for academic knowledge for the lower economic classes but, rather, to indoctrinate them toward acceptable [British] thinking and behavior. There was considerable consistency of educational philosophy among the promoters of public education throughout the provinces because the promoters were in contact with each other about their objectives.[111]

Today, students in Canada attend school for 192 days each year. They have eight-nine weeks vacation in the summer, two weeks vacation at Christmas and two weeks vacation for spring break. The school day usually lasts from about 8:30 a.m. to 3:00 p.m. from Monday through Friday. It is recommended that homework be assigned ten minutes per grade, which means that, by sixth grade, homework is assigned for sixty minutes each night and by eleventh grade, homework is assigned for one hundred ten minutes per night. Schools are free to alter this schedule and often do—to the upside. In Toronto, in 2008, Canada's largest school board seriously considered eliminating homework during holidays and long weekends because of growing concern against a "culture of homework that critics say is ruining family life." All provinces do not follow the same schedule but they are similar.[112]

One in sixteen children, or 6.3 percent of the school population in Canada, attends private school and it is difficult to gain entrance into many of these schools.[113] Because they are so selective, private schools can dismiss students for any behavioral or academic problems. Therefore, in general, private schools in Canada are even more disciplined and more academically demanding than public schools. Once again, it appears that the higher quality of education in Canada, as compared to the United States, may be accounted for by Time on Task.

Chapter 6
The TOTIL Method of Education
(Time on Task Independent Learning)

As previously mentioned, consideration of educational and psychological research, including my own, and personal experience from over twenty years of teaching at all levels leads me to the inescapable conclusion that Time on Task (TOT) is, by far, the most important variable for a superior education. Other variables are important only insofar as they contribute to Time on Task. However, one variable has additional value. This is the Independent Learning (IL), learner-centered method embodied in the TOTIL method. In addition to increasing Time on Task, the learner-centered method results in individuals who can teach themselves any concept—any time—any place. In so doing, students learn to think and to reason. A combination of TOT and IL results in the most effective and efficient method of education possible, that is, a student gets the most learning for the least amount of time spent in the endeavor.

The TOTIL method is not really new. This was the way most people learned in past generations, including our founding fathers and other colonists. People deviated from this independent learning/self teaching method primarily because of a lack of books and other materials. Because books were very rare and extremely expensive, children were herded into classes and teachers were hired to read the one available book or manuscript, or to gain knowledge from elsewhere, and then explain the concepts to several or many students at once. Once this teacher-centered method became ingrained, it created a culture of dependency on teachers. Parents and students believed they were necessary, and authorities had power over students and parents that they did not want to relinquish.

TOT (Time on Task) encourages students to work hard. IL (Independent Learning) encourages students to work smart, that is, more effectively and efficiently. If students do not have to focus on schoolwork for twelve-fifteen hours a day, as is the case in most of the high-performance Asian and KIPP-type schools, they will have more time to socialize with peers and/or become involved in other desirable pursuits, including interacting with family members. Below are the most important features of the TOTIL method.

To maximize Time on Task the student does not interact with others while studying. However, whether the student is being schooled at home or in a group situation, someone should be present to make sure the student sticks to the task. The monitor is not there to teach, just to supervise. The monitor should not answer questions. If there are to be multiple students in a room, each child should be assigned to his or her own cubicle or space so that interaction is not possible.

The student is the teacher. The best way for anyone to learn a subject or a concept is to teach it. To whom? To himself/herself. How? By utilizing the best materials that have been or can be developed. This is absolutely essential and will be discussed in the next chapter. Once children learn how to learn, they becomes academically self-reliant and independent. This adds enormously to self esteem and encourages more learning.

Most learning at the undergraduate level, and even more so at the graduate level, is done through self teaching. Upon entering college many students complain that college teachers are lazy and do not teach; they just present the material and the student is expected to learn it. It is true that most college teachers do not teach much. By this time, students are expected to be able to teach themselves. It is unfortunate that students are not expected to do this earlier. Adapting to self teaching in college can be overwhelming and many students drop out of colleges or universities because they cannot adapt. They are too academically dependent.

Begin the child's education as soon as he or she is ready. Children cannot engage in Independent Learning until they know how to read, write their letters and work with basic numbers. This is usually possible at about age three or four. Some children can learn these skills from videos. Others may learn from parents or reading teachers. The problem with hiring teachers for this task is that most children at this age have a very limited attention span— probably about fifteen minutes. Therefore, study periods need to be spaced throughout the day.

The phonetic method should be used to teach reading. Games can be used to teach numbers and addition and subtraction. For example, games with dice are very helpful. The child counts the dots, then adds the dots on two or more dice together and eventually gets faster and faster. As soon as children can perform these basic skills and will attend to the task for a minimum amount of time, they are ready for an Independent Learning/self-teaching homeschool or group situation.

Students move at their own pace according to their ability. Many schools, especially private schools, claim to allow academically gifted students to move ahead according to their ability. In reality, this is almost never accomplished. Enrichment assignments are usually just busy work and students know it. The teacher is not able to handle several students at different levels unless some of them are working independently.

The self pacing of the TOTIL method encourages many children to learn much faster, and it also prevents students from being bored or being branded a "nerd" or a "dummy" because other children do not know their level unless they choose to tell them. Children of below-average intelligence also benefit from this method. They do not have to move as quickly as others. They are ready when they are ready.

The school calendar for the TOTIL method is as follows: six hours a day, including lunch, six days a week and ten and a half months a year. The school year can be extended if the parent prefers. Studying on Saturdays and minimum time off during the summer and at other times maintains the flow and helps prevent forgetting. Children should be encouraged to engage in social and physical activities after lessons have been completed. Such activities are very important for healthy physical and psychological development.

Primary subjects to be learned during the six-hour study period are mathematics, English grammar, writing and reading. Science and social studies are learned during the reading period and, to a lesser extent, during the grammar and writing period. At the elementary level this can be done informally through self-selected books. Later, carefully selected, self-teaching textbooks can be used if the parent or student prefers. The school day is as follows:

8:30 a.m. - 10:30 a.m.	mathematics
10:30 a.m. - 12:00 a.m.	English grammar and writing
12:00 p.m. - 12:30 p.m.	lunch
12:30 p.m. - 2:30 p.m.	reading

With this schedule the more difficult subjects will be presented in the morning when students are more mentally alert. Although this daily schedule may be mildly adjusted as desired, such as beginning earlier or later, it should be followed on a regular basis, Homework should be unnecessary.

Breakfast should be adequate and nutritious. For students to be at their best mentally, it is advisable for them to refrain from ingesting substances that might make them inclined to be more tense or lethargic, for example, sugar and caffeine. When I was a practicing psychologist, one of my specialties was anxiety disorders, including phobias, especially agoraphobia. I began by suggesting to patients that they refrain from ingesting anxiety-producing substances, including caffeine, sugar, over the counter antihistamines, alcohol, and even anti-anxiety medication or anti-depressive medication (with a physician's approval) whenever possible. When patients stated that they could not possibly give up such things, I told them that I was much less likely to be able to cure their anxieties or phobias. They needed to begin the necessary desensitization process at a zero level of anxiety, or as close as they could get to zero. This was proven to be the most effective way to proceed over and over again whenever patients deviated from the regimen.

A comment regarding Ritalin for Attention Deficit Disorder (ADD) is in order. When I was Director of Psychology and a member of the teaching faculty at a well-known hospital in Michigan, one of my assignments was to evaluate children whose parents, teachers or physicians suspected might have ADD, as well as some children who had already been diagnosed as having ADD. If a diagnosis of ADD was determined, Ritalin was to be administered.

I did not find a single child among the many I examined whom I determined should be prescribed Ritalin. These children were mostly behavioral problems or normally active children bored with the school regimen. This made many people upset and angry, especially the parents of the children who were already taking Ritalin. The excessive misbehavior of children immediately after they are removed from Ritalin is often deemed to be proof that Ritalin is necessary. However, this is usually a withdrawal symptom. Ritalin is a very powerful drug. I really did sympathize with these parents and teachers but the solution to the problem is not to drug children for years.

The six-hour TOTIL schedule, including lunch, may be modified on Saturdays by eliminating the reading lesson. If preferred, Sundays can be substituted for Saturdays to accommodate the needs or desires of a particular family. Also, the six weeks vacation during the year may be taken anytime the family desires. Some families will prefer the traditional holiday vacation, winter vacation, spring vacation and a shortened summer vacation schedule. Other families may prefer to take vacation time at Hanukkah, Ramadan, when mom or dad can easily get their vacations from work, when prices or crowds are better at certain vacation spots, or any other time of their choosing. Since students are teaching themselves, monitors in a TOTIL group setting do not have to be accommodated the same way teachers do in a public or private school setting. Monitors or supervisors can also take vacations during the year. Substitutes can be hired for them. This way the study groups function for the convenience of the parents, not the monitors/supervisors.

Care needs to be taken when considering the learning of social studies. When the ideas of various economic and political systems of government and secular and religious philosophies are introduced, children should read original source materials first. Then, they should read non-original source materials that are in favor of, not opposed to, the concept they are studying. Finally, students should study the writings of authors who disagree with the particular concept or philosophy. By this time, students should be well able to assess for themselves the validity of the newly introduced concept. It should be clear what philosophy is being promoted, unlike most school texts that promote particular philosophies in a surreptitious manner to indoctrinate children.

It is best to include all forms of each discipline, such as the following for political systems: constitutional republics, socialist/progressive systems, dictatorships, monarchies, theocracies and oligarchies. For economic systems, both Keynesian economics and Austrian economics should be included.

A reasonably thorough study of religious philosophies should include the following, most popular, world religions: Christianity, Islam, Hinduism, Judaism, Jainism and Buddhism (not originally considered a religion, but rather, a secular philosophy). I would also include Zoroastrianism, a classical Persian religion, for historical reasons. The Parsis are thought to have been the initiators of the first monotheistic religion and to have significantly influenced several current large religions.

A study of secular, that is, non-theistic, philosophies should probably include the following: Aristotle, Plato, Socrates, Confucianism (sometimes considered to be theistic), secular Humanism and Objectivism. There are many more that can be added according to the twishes or beliefs of the parents or interest of the students. Or, parents may choose to have their children ignore any of the philosophies mentioned above if they deem knowledge of such philosophies to be detrimental to their child's development. However, although not as important as, *"Know Thyself,"* the well-known Greek aphorism, *"Know Your Enemy"* from Sun Tzu's *The Art of War* is also very important advice for both intellectual and physical protection.

By the time the student has finished calculus—at about the equivalent of the tenth grade— sciences such as biology, physics, chemistry, geology and astronomy can be formally introduced using college-level textbooks. However, some parents or students may decide to have the student enter college at this point. Most will certainly be academically ready.

Extra-curricular activities can be introduced at any time. These include: music lessons, art lessons, foreign language lessons or anything else in which a child has an interest. However, these subjects are not part of the six-hour TOTIL academic curriculum.

As a former foreign language teacher for more than twenty years at all levels and to all age groups, there are a few recommendations I would like to make regarding the study of foreign languages. Many programs and teachers state that "you should learn a foreign language the way you learned your own language" and "use the immersion technique because it worked so well for the U.S. Army." I said this to my students many, many times. It certainly appears to make sense, but I was wrong and so are the others.

You cannot and should not try to learn the foreign language as you did your own language. You already know another language and it can help you to learn a new one more quickly. You cannot consider most methods an immersion method "like the Army used" because you are not immersing yourself in it. Immersion means speaking it all day, every day, and preferably without the interference of another language. I realize that bi-lingual families do not do this. This is quite different. Students in such situations are being constantly exposed to both languages.

Many years ago, a friend of mine, a nuclear engineer named Bob, needed to learn French so that he could move to France to work at a nuclear reactor station. Bob's company paid for him to take a course at the Berlitz Language School, which was using the "immersion" method – one hour per session, three times a week. The teachers were not allowed to use any English whatsoever and they were monitored to make sure they adhered to this rule. Whenever I saw Bob and asked about his progress, he was very discouraged. He just couldn't learn it. Finally, one week when I asked about his progress, he said he was going to quit even though he very much needed to know the language for his job.

The next time I saw Bob, I asked if he had quit. He smiled broadly and said no. He told me that it was going just fine and he was really learning. I asked what had happened. Did he finally just begin to catch on? He said no. He said the teacher had begun to silently pass him notes in English with the translations on it and he responded the same way with questions in English. Of course, the goal in learning a foreign language is to eventually think in the language. However, at the beginning, translating from English to the foreign language is automatic. One does it internally and trying to pretend one is not doing it is not helpful. This is not the currently accepted method but I have found that it works best.

My parents, who were bilingual, French and English, realized that all my French-speaking cousins were being disadvantaged, both personally and professionally. While they could speak both languages, they were not really literate in either and they had an accent that was considered undesirable professionally and socially. For these reasons, my parents decided to send my siblings and me to an English school and to cease speaking French whenever we were around. We did not grow up bilingual. It is possible that a better solution might have been to study the grammar of both languages and to have become more literate in both, but this was not being done in the schools, and my parents believed that this would take too much time from other subjects they considered more important.

I believe that students should first learn the basic grammar of a foreign language so that they know where the various parts of speech should be fitted into the sentence. It does not matter if you have memorized thousands of vocabulary words and pronounce them well if you do not know how to correctly form sentences and do not understand when someone speaks to you in the language.

It is very difficult to learn to speak a foreign language just by taking language classes, even if, supposedly, only the foreign language is spoken, which is rarely the case. Students often attend language classes for four or even five years in high school and their parents are surprised that they cannot speak the language. With twenty-five to thirty-five students in a class, how often do you think they get to speak even a single sentence? They not only do not get an opportunity to speak the language in class, they resist doing so very aggressively. American students are at a disadvantage relative to foreign language learning. In most other countries, especially Europe, a student can take a week-end vacation and speak another language most of the time. This is not the case in the United States.

After individuals have learned the rudiments of a language from grammar books, they can learn to speak from one of the commercial language courses through the use of CD's or DVD's. I prefer the Pimsleur CD's. It is essential to speak out loud when practicing a language. This greatly reduces inhibition about speaking, which is the biggest problem of all in learning a foreign language.

After learning basic grammar and using tapes to learn to speak the foreign language, if at all possible, the student should go to a country where that language is native and speak it exclusively for as long as possible, at least a month. This may be expensive but it is probably less so, and certainly must less time consuming, than spending several more years using tapes, attending classes, etc.

In sum, the proper sequence for learning a foreign language is as follows: first, grammar and translation; then, speaking and reading. Once again we go back to old methods to find the best way to learn something new.

Socialization is important. Many parents object to homeschooling or to the TOTIL method or any other self-taught method because they believe the children are not being socialized enough. Having taught in various schools, public and private, for over twenty years, and having practiced as a psychologist for just as many, I strongly believe that the disadvantages, both social and academic, of forced socialization in a regular public or private school setting far outweigh the advantages. Children are not able to pick their own associates or to avoid those with whom they do not wish to associate, often because of psychological or physical bullying. Most parents would be very anxious if they knew just how much physical and psychological danger their children face every day. More on this later.

In addition, children learn the values and habits of those with whom they associate, including the use of drugs or alcohol, gutter language, bullying, disrespect for authority, etc. This is true whether the school is a public school, a parochial school or an expensive private school. Yes, they will encounter these problems later in life, but by that time they will be better able to handle them. Socialization and academic learning are both important. But when done together, socialization is just interference or worse.

Since students will be finished with their academic studies early in the afternoon using the TOTIL method, and homework is not necessary, there will be plenty of time left for socialization through group activities such as sports, group games, swimming lessons, tennis lessons, music groups, art groups, etc. In a TOTIL group setting, the children will already be together for such activities. If they are alone in a homeschool setting, they can easily get together with other homeschoolers.

Relative to sports and other children's activities, it is best to let children make all the arrangements for themselves. Sports teams where the parents do all the organizing, teaching and selecting are of greatly reduced benefit to children. Yes, the child-centered method will probably be more haphazard and competitive than teams that are picked by parents who are careful not to hurt any feelings, but it is more instructive, more realistic and more gratifying to the children. During a soccer practice I was observing, I commented to the coach about the fact that the teams were not keeping score. He said that, since the children were only seven years old, the adults did not want to make the less competent children feel inferior. "However, he added as he smiled slightly, "the children do keep score mentally. They know exactly who did what and who the best players are."

As is true when a child is taught the basics of reading, writing and counting before moving on to Independent Learning, a child can gain advantage in being taught the basics of non-academic skills. I suggest such basics be taught by lessons that are as close together as possible. For example, in learning to swim, play tennis or a musical instrument, etc., children should be taught five times a week, rather than once a week. Too much forgetting occurs with the latter method. Then get out of the way and let them practice. Remember Bill Gates and the Beatles? After they learned the basics, it was practice they needed, not help.

Technical Education. It is preferable that children who do not wish to attend college or a university complete at least the equivalent of the eighth grade (and preferably the tenth or twelfth grade) in an academic setting using the TOTIL method. By then, they will have a good general education and will be able to think and to reason.

The ancients, for example, the Greeks and Romans, studied literature, Greek, Latin and rhetoric at the elementary level because, at that time, those were the best subjects to teach one to think and to reason. These subjects did not necessarily relate to what the students did for a career later, although rhetoric was important for anyone who wanted to become a leader and needed to convince others to do what he wanted them to do.

Students who do not wish to continue with an academic education will have many options to choose from because of their TOTIL background. They may wish to attend a technical school; become involved in a trade or an apprenticeship; start a business; or enter the workforce immediately.

The primary objective of undergraduate and graduate students is to continue learning and/or to obtain credentials that will enable them to acquire the kind of career they would like to pursue. Ten or twelve years of the TOTIL method will enable students to earn good scores in any examination they may need to take for college acceptance or placement, such as, the *Scholastic Aptitude Test* (SAT), the *ACT Test* and the *College Board Advanced Placement Tests* (AP). Passing AP tests will allow students to place out of several subjects and they may be able to finish an undergraduate degree in two or three years.

Chapter 7
Materials for the TOTIL
Method of Education.

As I stated previously, an essential ingredient for the success of the TOTIL (Time on Task Independent Learning) method is the utilization of excellent materials that present the concepts to be learned in such a manner that the student does not need to ask for help from anyone else, that is, in an incremental, hierarchical manner with constant review. The Saxon Math books combined with the Saxon Language Arts books (Saxon Grammar and Writing books), a good dictionary and a library card, satisfies this requirement extremely well.

The Saxon Math books progress from first or second grade, depending on the child's reading level, through high school calculus. I have never been more impressed with any textbook or academic materials. These books were written by Stephen Hake and John Saxon.

Because I was so impressed with the Saxon math materials, I decided to use them to teach math to my grandson, Spencer Ball, who was in Kindergarten (five years old, one year early). At the time, Spencer knew how to read, knew his numbers from one-one hundred, could add and subtract single digits and could also print, but not well.

Spencer and I began with *Saxon Math Homeschool 5/4* which is considered to be appropriate for fourth to fifth grade students in public and private elementary schools and second grade for self-taught or homeschooled children. The kit contains three separate books: the textbook, a test and worksheet book, and a solutions manual/answer book.

Each chapter of the textbook is divided into four sections as follows:

<u>Warm Up</u> – This section includes practice of previously learned basic skills (addition, subtraction, multiplication or division), a mental math problem and a problem-solving exercise that elicits strategies for solving difficult problems. The latter is excellent for developing reasoning ability.

<u>New Concept</u> – This section is introduced and explained very clearly so the student can understand without help. I did not realize this before I began and was amazed. Spencer did not need my help. Examples are then used to demonstrate the new concept.

<u>Lesson Practice</u> – This section contains problems that practice the new concept.

<u>Mixed Practice</u> – This section contains problems that practice concepts from all previous chapters. Each problem number has a small, italicized number after it which indicates the chapter where the concept was first introduced. As a result, the student can review it, if necessary. This is my favorite feature.

This last feature in the Mixed Practice section, together with the clarity and simplicity of the presentation of the New Concept enabled Spencer to read and interpret the material without help. After a few lessons, I realized that my only function was to motivate him to continue. As a teacher I was superfluous. This is when I first realized that young children could, in fact, teach themselves. Thank you, Spencer!

Tests are given every five chapters. Since answers/solutions are given in a separate book, parents or monitors can give the test to students when they are ready, or students can keep them if they can be trusted not to look at the answers until after the test has been taken.

The Saxon philosophy of stressing incremental development and continual review is different from most other math textbooks which introduce a concept and then often do not present it again for several chapters. By this time, students have likely forgotten the concept and need someone to explain it (or think they do), because, unlike the Saxon textbook, they do not have numbers before each problem indicating the chapter where the concept was first introduced and explained.

Spencer and I worked together, on the telephone only, for eighteen hours total, in twenty-minute increments, three times a week, over a period of six weeks. No additional time was spent on homework or other projects. Spencer finished one third of the book, that is, forty chapters in this time period. However, we did skip some of the Warm Up exercises because the study sessions were so short. I would definitely not recommend skipping any exercises in regular sessions.

Due to time constraints, Spencer was not able to continue our sessions. Once he had mastered the multiplication tables, he needed to have more frequent sessions so that he would not forget between sessions. As stated earlier, keeping time periods away from task at a minimum is very important. This is why it is important to study six days a week and have as little vacation time as possible.

Following is a partial list of concepts that were mastered by five-year-old Spencer in this eighteen-hour time period:

Addition – Multiple Digits

Subtraction – Multiple Digits

Multiplication – The Multiplication Table through the 10's

Division – Single Digits

Missing Addends in Addition and Subtraction (Basic Algebraic Equations)

Place Value, Writing Numbers through 999,999,999

Number Lines, Gauges, Thermometers, Scales, Clocks

Linear System of Measurement – U.S. Customary System and Metric System

Capacity/Volume – U.S. Liquid Measures, Metric Liquid Measures

Lines, Segments, Rays

Basic Geometric Concepts – Perimeter, Area, Radius, Diameter, Identification of Various Angles and Triangles
Fractions, Mixed Numbers, Decimals

I think it is obvious that Spencer learned much, much more in eighteen hours of Individual Learning than he would have learned in a classroom with other children. Time on Task. I think most people would be very distressed if they realized how much time is wasted in a regular classroom setting. Although Spencer is of above average intelligence, I.Q. is not particularly important for the TOTIL method to succeed. Students will get there when they get there, that is, at their own pace. No teacher is needed or desired—just someone who will make sure the child is attending to the lesson. However, it is extremely important that each student be able to sit and work quietly without disturbing other children and without excessive monitoring.

After the success I had using the *Saxon Math Homeschool 5/4* book with Spencer, I longed for Saxon language arts books, using the same method, to complete the self-teaching curriculum I was considering. About a year later, I discovered that Saxon had developed such a set of books: *Grammar and Writing 5; Grammar and Writing 6; Grammar and Writing 7; and Grammar and Writing 8.* These were written by Christie Curtis and Mary Hake. I decided to test them immediately.

Grammar and Writing 5, the first language arts book in the series, is recommended for fifth grade students. However, knowing that homeschool or self-taught students could begin *Saxon Math Homeschool 5/4* in the second grade, I decided to test this book on second graders. I contacted a friend who is a second grade teacher in a public school in California and asked him to give the first two lessons to his class. Steve said he would like to do this but that children do not learn to read for information until the fourth grade and so, most of them, or perhaps all of them, would not understand the instructions for the exercises. I had not considered this. But I later discovered that this is a common assumption. A few days later I saw Barbara Bush, wife of ex-president George H.W. Bush, on television. She was discussing education and mentioned that from Grade 1 to Grade 3 children learn to read and from Grade 4 they read to learn.

To test this theory, I decided to go back to Spencer, who by this time was six years old and in second grade (one year early). I handed him the first two lessons of *Grammar and Writing 5* and told him that I did not want to give him any instructions because I wanted to determine if he could understand them by himself. I instructed him to write down the time he began and the time he finished and, if he could not do the exercises, to just let me know.

Thirty-five minutes later, Spencer came downstairs. I said, "What's the matter, honey, couldn't you do it?"

He responded, "I have finished."

Surprised, I said, "Well, then, let's check the answers." We did, and they were all correct.

Realizing that Spencer is not an academically average student, I decided to have my friend, Steve, give the exercises in the first lesson (both math and grammar) to his class of second graders in a lower-economic, multicultural, public school. I also gave the first two grammar assignments to a fourth grader in public school. The fourth grader completed the assignment in twenty-two minutes (both lessons) with all answers correct. The public school second graders were not timed. They did fairly well on the Saxon Math lesson but not at all well on the Saxon Grammar and Writing lesson. Remember that *Saxon Math Homeschool 5/4* is intended for fourth graders in public school and *Saxon Grammar and Writing 5* is intended for fifth graders in public school. The difference between the two lessons (math and grammar) and between the students was immediately apparent. The intelligence of the student was not particularly important, nor was the grade level. The important difference was how well the student could read. A higher reading level was necessary for the grammar and writing lesson than for the arithmetic lesson. For most of the students who did poorly on the math lesson, English was not their native language. Most others performed extremely well.

I am convinced that almost all students, at any grade level or age, will do well with the Saxon materials if they can read reasonably well. Some would just have to read the instructions several times. Determining ahead of time that students cannot follow written instructions until Grade 4 is the beginning of teaching them to be academically dependent on others.

Before beginning the first Saxon math book, *Saxon Math Homeschool 5/4* or the first Saxon grammar and writing book, *Grammar and Writing 5*, it would be best if the parent or monitor/child-care worker would read the Preface and then explain Lesson One to the child. The Preface is more difficult to understand than the rest of the book and the child needs to understand the structure of the book in order to use it properly. For example, at the very beginning of each lesson in the book, *Grammar and Writing 5,* there are the words "dictation" and "journal entry" on top of the page. The Preface explains how to handle the journal entry. It also informs the student that there is a dictation at the back of the textbook which they need to copy and then practice before each new lesson until the next test. As part of the test, the parents or monitors will dictate this paragraph to the students, individually, who will copy it and then correct it themselves. Students learn spelling and punctuation primarily through these dictation exercises. An explanation of the first lesson and the dictation exercises are the only times the student will need help from someone else.

After having searched for many years, the Saxon books were the very best I could find. If a parent finds other books or teaching materials that they prefer to the Saxon books, of course they can use these with the TOTIL method instead. This method is not dependent on any particular materials, although they do need to be self-explanatory.

As I have stated previously, the learning of foreign languages is not part of the six-hour TOTIL method of education. However, I would like to mention some of the materials I have found to be extremely helpful in learning foreign languages. The first book to be acquired should be the *AMSCO Workbook, Spanish (French, German) First Year (Two Years, Three Years).* This is an excellent grammar book which promotes incremental development and constant review. It presents each new concept clearly and then gives exercises to practice it in ascending order of difficulty.

The *Pimsleur* language CD's can be used concurrently with the *AMSCO Workbook* to learn to speak the language. Sentences are presented in English and time is left for the student to repeat them in the foreign language. The correct translation and pronunciation is then presented in the foreign language. Students will not progress or lose their fear of speaking in the language if they do not say each translation out loud.

A *Cuthbertson* verb wheel should also be used in learning a foreign language. This is a circular, rotatable disc mounted on a piece of thin cardboard seven inches square that lists all the irregular verbs in the language and presents all the tenses for each verb on the front. It also contains all of the tenses of the regular verbs on the back of the wheel. It is quite compact and can be carried anywhere.

It is essential for students to have appropriate materials for any subject or skill they wish to learn. This shortens the learning period and keeps the student interested.

Chapter 8
Comparison of the Learner-Centered Method of Education and the Teacher-Centered Method of Education

Teacher-centered academic education for Grades K-12 is obsolete, as is most teacher-centered education. It is undesirable—academically, psychologically, physically and financially. We have seen that, with this method, in order to achieve a reasonable level of academic success, a student must spend many, many hours each day schooling, that is, being involved in school related tasks, including studying or pretending to do so. For example, students in academically superior nations, as ranked through the PISA international tests, are involved in schooling from 7:30 a.m. to midnight. KIPP students in America, also known for academic excellence, as mentioned in the movie *Waiting for Superman* attend school from 7:30 a.m. until 5:00 p.m. each week day and then spend two and one half to three hours at home studying. That is about twelve hours schooling each school day for KIPP students and twelve-fifteen hours schooling each school day for the high-ranking PISA students. How much of that time do you think is spent actually thinking? These are children.

Most children in the United States and most other western or undeveloped or semi-developed countries spend much less time in schooling or in Time on Task than do students from the high ranking PISA nations or KIPP-type schools. That is why the former perform much worse academically. For example, a regular school day in most American public and private, including parochial, schools lasts about seven hours and, for much of that time, students are not involved in academic pursuits. They are involved in schooling, but not studying. Other activities include: non-academic courses, lunch, homeroom, study-hall (where no one studies), assemblies, pep rallies, visits to the counselor, etc. In addition, if students become physically involved with hands-on activities, or socially involved by interacting with peers or the teacher (which is unavoidable), even less learning occurs. How much do you think these students are actually learning?

It is not how many hours students study or pretend to study that matters. It is how well they are actually processing information during that time that matters. How involved are the students mentally? Five and one half hours actively involved in the learning process with TOTIL, or another effective, learner-centered approach, is worth much, much more than seven hours in an American public or private school. It is also worth at least as much as twelve-fifteen hours in a high-performing Asian school using a teacher-centered, group-oriented, approach with the student's mind wandering much of the time. What is your attention span with someone, a teacher or speaker, talking to you for hours with numerous distractions from others? Think about the business conferences or meetings you have attended.

In addition to the academic problems inherent in a teacher-centered, group-oriented, setting, there are also psychological and physical problems. Most of us are aware of the damage of psychological bullying, which can be so severe that students spend their school years being tormented and some even resort to suicide. Most of us are also aware that a student can also be in physical danger in a public school setting where misbehaving children cannot be dismissed— anything from having lunch money taken on a daily basis to being psychologically or physically assaulted or killed. This problem is not restricted to low-income schools.

I remember an eleventh-grade student I "taught" in a very academically oriented public school in an upper economic class neighborhood. After a few weeks in class, he proudly showed me a drawing he had made depicting a large box with blood dripping down the side. He said his mother was in it and that he had killed her. There were people standing around wearing swastika arm bands with a Star of David on them. It did not require a licensed psychologist, which I was, to infer that this child was dangerous. I went to the principal and told him about the situation.

His response was, "I know he is probably dangerous. Every teacher he has had told me the same thing."

I said, "Then why don't you get rid of him?"

He replied, "I can't. I have tried. The court won't let me."

Most people are not aware that administrators cannot expel students who are paranoid schizophrenics, sociopaths, addicted to drugs, either prescribed or not prescribed, or just plain malevolent, until they have actually done something really egregious—and then it is too late. Also, in some school systems, teachers are not allowed to interfere in fights between students, even if one is being beaten. In addition, trying to enlist a parent's help with his own child can be a problem. Several times I tried to help parents by informing them that their child had a problem, usually drugs, so we would be able to work together to help the student. In most instances, the parents refused to listen and threatened to sue me if I ever mentioned it again, either to them or to anyone else. In many cases, I quit trying to help.

When I read in a newspaper or see on television that a student has viciously attacked and/or killed someone and other students or teachers or administrators say, "I never would have imagined that" or "I didn't see it coming," I tend not to believe them. Chances are that many people knew, but they did not want to get into trouble by saying so. Also, school personnel know that the primary goal in public schools is to keep students in school, no matter what, so that the school district can get the money for them from the government and/or the child can graduate because "a diploma is necessary for success in life." How much do you think they are learning if they do not want to be there, and how much do you think the other students are learning if they are being harassed or intimidated by such students? It is equivalent to being in a prison where the prisoner is subjected to all kinds of mistreatment with no way to escape. Any child deserves better.

Keeping children in school who do not want to be there and who will constantly disrupt and endanger other students is unfair to them, to the other students, to the teachers and to those who are paying for the education. I have often had people ask me, "Well, what would you do with the children not in school—put them out in the streets where they will likely get into trouble?" My response to that is that it is a better alternative than keeping them in school where they will disrupt, intimidate, bully, and possibly physically injure other students and keep them from getting the education they deserve.

An education should be considered a privilege, not a right, and one earns the privilege by paying attention and not depriving others of their education. What to do with the disruptors is a separate problem. Our problem is to protect children and to provide them with a superior education. The TOTIL method is my way of helping children to acquire an academically superior education with as little time and effort, and as few negative consequences, as possible.

I do not agree with the commonly held belief that two of the reasons for student failure are that teachers are not prepared well enough academically or that they lack motivation, which can be improved through some incentive, such as merit pay. In my twenty plus years of teaching at all levels, I have met many poor teachers and many more good teachers, but rarely have I met a teacher who was not academically prepared to teach his or her subject.

Relative to merit pay, I would like to relate my own experience. I had always believed strongly in the benefits of merit pay and then came an opportunity to see this hope realized. It was announced that our school system, one of the four best (academically and socio-economically) in the state of Michigan, was about to implement merit pay. It would start in two weeks. The principal called a meeting of all teachers and announced that he was in charge of deciding who would qualify for merit pay and who would not, and that the awards were quite limited. He then stated that merit pay would be reserved for teachers who would volunteer to coach team sports.

It is easy to understand what teachers are doing wrong to contribute to the diminishing academic success of students. They are pretending that they can do the impossible—that they can do a good job of teaching at the same time they are trying to socialize students by allowing them to interact, and perhaps also handle unruly students at the same time. In the past this was not quite as big a problem because students were not permitted to interact or misbehave. Most schools in foreign countries, especially Asian countries, still punish misbehaving children, often harshly. It is difficult to blame the teachers. If they tell the truth, they will not have a job. Insufficient teacher training or education is not the problem. Motivation of teachers is not the problem. It is the teacher-centered, student-interaction method that is wrong. It does not work.

Other professionals and other individuals are guilty of the same kind of deception. Psychologists pretend they can do the impossible. Judges send them clients/patients to "cure" or "fix." A husband who is beating his wife is sent for anger management so he will stop beating her. An addict is sent to have his addiction cured. The judge pretends he believes this will work so he is relieved of the responsibility of making a more difficult decision. The psychologist pretends this will work so s/he will get paid. The miscreant pretends this will work so s/he will not have to go to prison. Physicians and surgeons also pretend they can do things they cannot do, and they often wind up getting sued, not usually because of actual neglect on their part, but because patients have unrealistic expectations to which they contribute.

I have never met or counseled a patient who was cured because s/he was forced to get treatment. Patients must want to get better and become intimately involved in the process. This is rarely the case with referred patients. They invariably believe that someone else is at fault. The name of this game is "pass the responsibility on to someone else and never accept responsibility yourself."

I have not found any significant difference academically between public, private, or parochial school students. However, in parochial or other private schools that can dismiss students, the behavior tends to be slightly better. I attended parochial schools for many years and most of my siblings graduated from them. My own children graduated from public high schools and attended public and private universities. My grandchildren attend private elementary schools. The method is the same in all of them, that is, teacher-centered with student interaction, so the results are very similar.

Homeschooling is a bridge between the teacher-centered method and the learner-centered method. While there is usually at least one teacher involved in homeschooling (usually the parent), the student performs a good deal of the work independently, as s/he does in the TOTIL Method. Since there is usually only one child, or one family of children involved in homeschooling and the parents are there to monitor them, there is much less social interaction in homeschooling than in a regular public or private school setting and, therefore, there is much more Time on Task. There is some difference in curriculum between the two methods, TOTIL and homeschooling, but many homeschooling families already use the all-important, self-teaching, Saxon math books.

Since the parents of homeschoolers have already taken the difficult and courageous step of moving away from dependence on the public or private school systems, it should be relatively easy for them to adapt to the TOTIL method. This is especially true since the TOTIL method is much more efficient and convenient than the homeschooling method. With TOTIL the parent does not need to be involved in the teaching process—in fact, should not be involved. Also, more than one family can be included and parents can share the monitor/child care worker. This frees the parents for other pursuits and leads to more learning and independence for the students.

An excellent example of the success of the self-teaching method of education is that of Dr. Arthur Robinson's six children. Arthur Robinson, Ph.D. is a successful, internationally-known scientist who was the monitor/supervisor for his children. He provided a room with seven large desks, six for them and one for himself, and a roomful of materials that he and his deceased wife had collected for this purpose. The children taught themselves. Dr. Robinson did not answer questions. This self-teaching method was very successful. Dr. Robinson's children graduated two years early from undergraduate school, primarily because they had placed out of several subjects using the *Advanced Placement* (AP) tests. They have all obtained Ph.D.'s (one DVM), or are presently working on one, in various scientific fields, such as chemistry, nuclear engineering and veterinary medicine.[114]

Based on this experience, Dr. Robinson, some of his graduate students and his children developed the Robinson Curriculum for Grades K-12 (on twenty-two CD's), which also utilizes the Saxon math books. Many parents consider this to be an academically superior, convenient and inexpensive program. However, some parents may object to the fact that many of the books selected for reading in this curriculum are somewhat Christian oriented. Parents of other religious or non-religious orientations may prefer something different. Also, some parents believe that the reading materials are archaic; others consider them to be classic. It is a matter of personal preference.

The TOTIL method, or another effective, learner-centered method, is necessary to accommodate the demands of life in the more technologically-advanced society of the 21st century and beyond. Implementation of such a method will accomplish several desirable goals.

We will have a nation of graduates who are much better prepared academically and technologically. They will be better able to think and to reason. They will invent new devices, methods and technologies that can enrich and protect our lives. In addition, we will not have to import scientists, mathematicians and engineers from other countries. It is difficult to exaggerate the benefits of a better educated populace.

Parents who work or choose to live in foreign countries for extended periods will not have to concern themselves with finding a suitable school for their children to attend. Parents in both urban and suburban areas who take their children to school every day for safety and distance reasons, will no longer have to do so and will save a great deal of time, energy and expense.

Families will be free to live wherever they wish, including remote areas, without having to consider that their children may not easily be able to get to school. For example, in sparsely populated areas in Alaska a large percentage of students attend school every day by small airplanes, which usually can accommodate only one or two children at a time.

More time for family interaction and restructuring of time for families and society is possible with the TOTIL method. As a result of not having to be in a particular place at a particular time to accommodate school and teacher schedules, parents will be much more in control of their lives.

Public schools are also a danger to America's financial health. As a nation we spend tens of billions of dollars every year for a system that not only does not work, that is, students do not learn, but is detrimental to the academic, psychological and physical well-being of students. Many people are shocked when someone even suggests that the United States Federal Department of Education should be abolished. I was teaching in high school when President Carter established this department. Educational achievement immediately increased momentum on a downhill slide that has not yet stopped. More useless courses, rules and extra-curricular activities were initiated. Student behavior worsened as pressure was increased to keep children in school. I should make it clear that I was teaching in one of the four best public high schools in the state of Michigan, academically and socio-economically. Imagine what happened in other schools . However, since I had already taught in other schools, that is, public schools in Detroit, it is difficult to imagine that they could have gotten much worse.

As a nation, we could save tens of billions of dollars every year for financially-strapped taxpayers. We could eliminate all government educational agencies and hundreds of thousands of government bureaucrats at all levels—federal, state and local. We could eliminate public school personnel, including teachers, school administrators and counselors. We could eliminate school plants, that is, fancy buildings with auditoriums, swimming pools, etc.

Parents in local communities could be responsible for minimal regulation of education, or parents could be personally responsible for their own children. Such a lack of bureaucracy would also eliminate numerous rules and regulations that negatively affect learning. Students would be acquiring a much better education at much, much less cost. Competent teachers could turn their expertise into numerous other pursuits, including developing books and materials that would help students to teach themselves.

No, this is not impossible. Our founding fathers started this way, as did most other educationally oriented people. Most, if not all, of the reasons people changed from the learner-centered model to the teacher-centered mrthod are no longer valid. Because books were extremely rare and expensive, it was convenient to hire teachers who would read the books and then pass the information on to groups of students who were assembled for that purpose. Books and other materials are now readily available and printing of materials is inexpensive. Also, access to computers eliminates much of the need for libraries. Students can get a much better education than they are now getting for just a few hundred dollars a year, so poor students are not disadvantaged.

The beneficial academic, psychological, physical and financial improvements and personal freedom that the TOTIL method can bring are almost endless. We just have to overcome inertia and teacher dependence and be brave enough to take that first big step.

Chapter 9
Eight Steps to Follow to Implement the TOTIL Method of Education

Now it is time to act. By following the eight steps below, you can be assured that your children will receive a superior education, both quantitatively and qualitatively. They will learn twice as much in the time presently allotted for Kindergarten through high school. Also, they will be academically independent and self teachers of any subject—any time.

Step 1. Decide whether or not you want to accept the responsibility for your children's education. It is much more convenient to send them to a public, parochial, or other private school and let the professionals make the decisions. Remember, though, that you do not know how much they are learning; what they are being taught; or with whom they are associating. This is an especially difficult decision for families who do not have a stay-at-home parent. Free and/or convenient child care service is the primary reason most parents will not adopt this or any other self-teaching method.

You can more comfortably make this decision if you are first convinced that your child really can learn more with the learner-centered method. Test this theory. Get a copy of *Saxon Math Homeschool 5/4.* Have your child use it for one-half hour per day for a month. Do not help your child with the lessons. See what a difference it makes. If you are impressed, as I am sure you will be, proceed to Step 2.

Step 2. Decide whether you want your child to learn alone in your own home or in a group environment. If you prefer a group environment, have a few friends, neighbors or parents of your children's present schoolmates test the method as you did in Step 1. If necessary, you could even advertise locally. Be sure to include only children who do not have behavioral problems and are capable of working without excess supervision.

Step 3. If you have decided to have a group of students together, find a large room with large desks where the children can have privacy, that is, where they do not interact during the six-hour academic period, except for the half-hour lunch period.

Step 4. Decide if you (or another parent) want to act as monitor or if you want to hire a monitor/child care worker to do this. Remember, you are not doing the work, your child is. No help is needed or desired. The size of the group is up to you. Also, you can have several grade levels together. With the TOTIL method, it does not matter.

Step 5. Hire the monitor (if you have decided not to do this yourself). The only task this person will need to perform is to read the dictation exercise in *Grammar and Writing 5* to each child when he or she is ready to take the periodic tests—after every five lessons; or the parents can read the dictation to their child at their convenience.

The monitor does not have to be a teacher. However, I suspect that many retired teachers, new teachers without jobs, graduate students, etc. would be willing to monitor the children if they did not have to simultaneously teach and fight students, the administration, the teachers' union and government bureaucrats.

Step 6. Decide on a set of rules for all students to follow. The first rule should be that any student who misbehaves or is distracting in any way will be excluded until he or she decides to behave. Perhaps a private room can be used for time-out if the behavior is only temporary. You will be surprised how many potentially disruptive students will behave well when others are behaving well; when they are involved in the activity; and when they have to earn the privilege of staying.

Step 7. Get a set of Saxon math books, Saxon grammar and writing books, a good dictionary, a thesaurus and a library card for each child. For all children in grade equivalents one-five, I would begin with the *Saxon Math Homeschool 5/4* kit, which is considered to be appropriate for fourth to fifth grade students in public or private schools and second grade for self-taught or homeschool students. I would also get the *Saxon Grammar and Writing 5* kit for all students in grade equivalents three-eight. Some students can handle this in the second grade. It is dependent upon the reading level of the student. The older math students will benefit from the review and will not miss any concepts as they move up to Saxon calculus. However, it may not be necessary for them to do all the basic review exercises at the beginning of the chapters. The older grammar and writing students will get more experience in English composition and grammar. Some first and second grade students may have to work extra hard at the beginning, but it will get easier quickly. Remember, Spencer used *Saxon Math Homeschool 5/4* in Kindergarten and he was younger than usually allowed for this grade.

As stated previously, I recommend that the parent or monitor/ child care worker explain the first lesson of each of the Saxon sets of books, that is, *Saxon Math 5/4* and *Grammar and Writing 5*, so that the child understands the structure of the book and what is expected. All following lessons in both sets of books follow the same structure so this only needs to be done once.

Step 8. Be sure you are operating in accordance with the rules of the state and country in which the schooling will take place. In California, for example, you must file a *Private School Affidavit* (PSA) with your local county board of education. This must be done by October for the following year. The following excerpt regarding private schools in California is from *Home School Association of California, Frequently Asked Questions* and is a quote from the California Education Code.

> Many California families choose to comply with the state's compulsory attendance law by establishing a private school in their own home. These families file the private school affidavit (see section 33190) with their local county board of education... Since the Education Code allows anyone to establish a private school of any size, with any philosophy, employing whatever teachers they choose, parents use this legal provision to homeschool.

> The private school affidavit is a simple form that notifies the

state of the existence of a private school. It is not a license given by the state. The state does not approve, evaluate, recognize, endorse, or supervise your private school in any way. The affidavit is merely a device by which the Department of Education's Demographics Unit keeps track of the number of school children in California.[115]

Not only do I believe that our present educational system, the teacher-centered, group-oriented, socio-politically motivated method, does not work, I believe it cannot work. Independent Learning, that is, learner-centered, individually oriented, academically motivated education, leads to much more Time on Task and much more efficient and effective learning. Until we reject the teacher-centered method, our children will not learn to think independently and will not have the knowledge and skills necessary to function effectively in the world in which they live.

Now it is time for you to decide if you would prefer to raise a child who will acquire an outstanding academic or technical education and who is self-confident, self-reliant, independent and able to think and reason, or a child who is unable to compete with children from other countries who are much better educated academically and who will be their superiors professionally.

Go ahead. Take the plunge. One giant step forward to academic excellence and freedom!

Endnotes

Chapter 1

1. *Programme for International Student Assessment*, 6-7. (http://en.wikipedia.org/wiki/Programme_for_International_Student_Assessment)
2. Veronique de Rugy, *Reason,* "Losing the Brains Race," March 2011, 18.
3. *Programme,* 6 – 7.
4. Hedrick Smith, *Making Schools Work*, KIPP: Mike Feinberg Interview, 1, (http://www.pbs.org/making schoolswork/sbs/kipp/feinberg.html)
5. *Dream Big*, 1, (http://www.kippadelante.org)
6. Ibid.
7. *KIPP: FAQ*, 3, (http://www.kipp.org/about-kipp/faq)
8. Smith, Hedrick, *Making Schools Work.*
9. *Knowledge is Power Program*, 2, (http://en.wikipedia.org/wiiki/KIPP)
10. *KIPP: FAQ*, 3-4.
11. *KIPP: FAQ*, 2.
12. *KIPP: FAQ*, 4.

Chapter 2

13. *Programme,* 7.
14. de Rugy, Veronique, *Reason*, 18.
15. Dan Lips, Shanea Watkins, Ph.D., and John Fleming, *Does Spending More on Education Improve Academic Achievement?* Backgrounder,

#2179, 5-6, (http://www.heritage.org/research/reports/2008/09/ does-spending-more-on-education

16. *Poor Marks for U.S. Education System*, 2, (http://www.cbsnews.com/ stories/2002/11/26/world/main530872. html)

17. *Programme*, 7.

18. Eric A.Hanushek, Paul E. Peterson, and Ludger Woessmann, , *Teaching Math to the Talented*, 18, (www.educationnext.org)

19. Ibid.

20. *Programme*, 3.

Chapter 4

21. Tim Lambert, *A Brief History of Education*, 2, (http:/www. localhistories.org/education.html)

22. Mirium Balmuth, *Canadian Woman Studies*, Female Education in 16th & 17th Century England, 17-18, Vol. 9, Numbers 3 and 4, (http://pi.library.yorku.ca/ojs/index.php/cws/article/view/11719)

23. Lambert, Tim, *A Brief History*, 2 and 3.

24. Balmuth, Mirium, *Female Education*.

25. Lambert, Tim, *A Brief History*, 2-3, (http:/www.localhistories.org/ education.html)

26. Lambert, Tim, *A Brief History*, 3.

27. Deeptha Thattai, *A History of Public Education in the United States*, 5, (http://wwwlservintfree.net/~sidmn-ejournal/publications/2001-11/ PublicEducation)

28. Christina Meiss, *Benjamin Franklin*, 1-2, (http://www. nd.edu/~rbarger/www7/franklin.html)

29. *George Washington's Mount Vernon, A Brief Biography of George Washington: Childhood: 1732-1746*, 1-2, (http://www.mountvernon. org/learn/meet_george/index.cfm/ss/21)

30. *Signers of the Declaration of Independence, John Adams*, 2, 11/4/2010, (http://www.ushistory.org/declaration/signers/adams_j.htm)

31. *Signers of the Declaration of Independence, Thomas Jefferson*, 1, 11/4/2010, (http://www.ushistory.org/declaration/signers/jefferson. htm)

32. Robert Peterson, *Education in Colonial America*, September 1983, Volume: 33, Issue: 9, Presented in The Freeman: Ideas on Liberty, (www.thefreemanonline.org)

33. *Progressive Education*, 1, (http://en.wikipedia.org/wiki/Progressive_education)
34. *Progressive Education*, 2.
35. *Secondary education in the United States*, 3, (http://en.wikipedica.org/wiki/Secondary_education_in_the_United_States)
36. Christopher Koliba, *Democracy and Education, Schools and Communities Initiative, Conceptual Framework and Preliminary Findings*, (http://www.uvm.edu/~dewey/articles/Democonc.htm)

Chapter 5
37. *Programme*, 2.
38. Ibid., 6-7.
39. Ibid., 5-7.
40. Ibid., 5.
41. Ibid., 5-7.
42. *Education in the People's Republic of China*. 3-6, 16, (http://en.wikipedia.org/wiki/Education_in_the_People's_Republic_of_China)
43. Ibid., 1, 6.
44. Ibid., 3, 7.
45. Ibid., 9.
46. Ibid.
47. *Three die amid Gaokao* Test, 1, (http://english.peopledaily.com.cn/90001/90776/90776/90882/7018512.html)
48. *Education in the People's Republic*, 7.
49. Ibid., 10, 11, 16.
50. *Programme*, 6-7.
51. *Education in Singapore*, 1, (http://en.wikipedia.org/wiki/Education_in_Singapore)
52. Early Childhood Australia, *Starting school – a Singapore story told by children*, 2. (http://www.earlychildhoodaustralia.org.au/australian_journal_of_early_childhood/a
53. *Education in Singapore*, 3.
54. School Accountability Framework Review, National and International Perspectives and Approaches Research Papers - Detailed, *Singapore – Education System and School Accountability*, 3-4. September 2006.

55. Ibid., 8.
56. Anglo info, Singapore Local Reference Information, *School Holidays in Singapore*, 1, (http://singapore.angloinfo.com/information/20schoolhols.asp)
57. School Accountability Framework Review, *Singapore*, 3-4.
58. Early Childhood Australia, *Starting school*, 2.
59. *Programme*, 6-7.
60. *Education in Hong Kong*, 2, (http://en.wiki.pedia.org/wiki/Education_in_Hong_Kong)
61. Ibid., 4.
62. Ibid., 9.
63. Ibid., p. 4,
64. Ibid., 6.
65. *Programme*, 5-7.
66. Asian Info, *Historical Review of Korea's Education*, 2. (http://www.asianinfo.org/asianinfo/korea/education.htm)
67. *Education in South Korea*, 2-3. (http://en.wikipedia.org/wiki/Education_in_South_Korea)
68. *Education in South Korea*, 3-4.
69. Ibid.
70. Ibid.
71. Ibid., 4-5.
72. Ibid., 5-6.
73. Ibid., 7.
74. Ibid.
75. *Programme*, 6-7.
76. *Taiwan's Educational System*, 1, (http://www.saec.edutw/fulbright/sys-m-htm)
77. Ibid.
78. Ibid.
79. Ibid., 2.
80. *Programme*, 6-7.
81. *History of Education in Japan*, 1, (http://en.widkipedia.org/wiki/History-of-education-in-Japan)
82. Ibid., 2.
83. Ibid., 3.
84. Ibid.

85. Ibid.

86. Ibid.

87. Ibid., 4.

88. *Education in Japan,* 2, (http://countrystudies.us/japan/78.htm)

89. *A Day at School – Schools*, 1, (http://web-japan.org/kidsweb/explore/schools/q9.html)

90. *Japan - Primary and Secondary Education*, 1, (http:///78.htmcountrystudies.us/japan)

91. Ibid., 6.

92. *Education in Japan*, 7.

93. *Programme*, 5-7.

94. *Why do Finland's schools get the best results?* 1. (http://news.bbc.co.uk/2/hi/8601207.stm)

95. *Why Finland is First in Education*, 1, (http://www.suite101.com/content/why-finland-is-first-in-education-a96642)

96. *Education in Finland*, 2, (http://en.wikipedia.org/wiki/Education_in_Finland)

97. *Why do Finland's schools get the best results*? 2.

98. *Why Finland is First in Education*? 1.

99. *Why do Finland's schools get the best results?* 1.

100. *Why Finland is First in Education*, 2.

101. *Why does Finnish give better PISA results?* 1, (http://finnish-and-pisa.blogspot.com)

102. *Why do Finland's schools get the best results*? 2.

103. Ellen Gamerman, *What makes Finnish Kids So Smart?* 2, (http://online.wsj.com/article/SB120425355065601997.html)

104. *Why do Finland's schools get the best results?* 2.

105. *Why does Finnish give better PISA results?* 5, (http://finnish-and-pisa.blogspot.com)

106. *Programme*, 8.

107. Gamerman, Ellen, *What makes Finnish Kids So Smart*? 2.

108. *Programme*, 5-7.

109. *The Canadian Encyclopedia,* "Education, History of," 1, (http://www.thecanadianencyclopedia.com/PrinterFriendly.cfm?Params=A1ARTA)

110. Ibid., 2.

111. Ibid.

112. *Homework needs 'rethinking'*, 1-2, http://www.canada.com/topics/lifestyle/parenting/story.html?id=728f736f--a9d5-4c
113. *About Private Schools*, 1, (http://www.ourkids.net/school/about-private-schools.php)

Chapter 8
114. *Robinson Curriculum*, (http://www.robinsoncurriculum.com)

Chapter 9
115. *Home School of California, FAQ*, (http://www.hsc.org/index.php), 11/2/2010

Bibliography

Curtis, Christie and Hake, Mary, *Grammar and Writing 5,* Houghton, Mifflin Harcourt Publishers, Inc., Wilmington, 2010.

Cuthbertson, Stuart, Ph.D. and Cuthbertson, Lulu L., *The Cuthbertson Verb Wheels*, D.C. Heath and Company, 1933.

Gladwell, Malcolm, *Outliers: The Story of Success,* Little, Brown and Company, New York, 2008.

Hake, Stephen and Saxon, John, *Saxon Math Homeschool 5/4*, Saxon Publishers Inc., Wilmington, 2005.

Kounin, Jacob S., *Discipline and Group Management in Classrooms,* Kessinger Publishing Co., Whitefish, Montana, 1977.

Nazzi, Robert J., Bernstein, Bernard and Nuzzi, Theodore F., *Workbook in Spanish Three Years*, Amsco School Publications, Inc., Revised, New York , 1989.

Pimsleur, Paul, *Language Program*, Simon & Schuster Audio, New York and London, 1996.

Index

About The Author

Doris Leclerc Ball, Ph.D. is a retired teacher, psychologist, lecturer and researcher in psychology and education. Dr. Ball spent more than 40 years developing and refining the TOTIL Method—a revolution in educational methodology.

Dr. Doris and Mr. George Ball reside in San Diego, California. Their sons, Timothy Sams, Ph.D. and Eric Ball, Ph.D., also live in California with their families.

revolutionizingeducation@san.rr.com
revolutionizing education in america.com